felt craft fun

Dedication

This first one is for my children. I know I tell you this all the time, but here's physical proof that you really can do anything. I love you 3000.

Felt Craft Fun © 2025 by Jess DeVos and Better Day Books, an imprint of Schiffer Publishing, Ltd

Publisher: Peg Couch
Cover Designer: Lindsay Hess
Book Designers: Michael Douglas and Lori Ehrlich
Editors: Kaylee Schofield, Jules Hostetter, and Colleen Dorsey

Library of Congress Control Number: 2025930720

ISBN: 978-0-7643-7005-2
Printed in China
10 9 8 7 6 5 4 3 2 1

Published by Better Day Books, an imprint of Schiffer Publishing, Ltd.

Better Day Books
Email: hello@betterdaybooks.com
Web: www.betterdaybooks.com
Visit us on Instagram!
@better_day_books

Schiffer Publishing
4880 Lower Valley Road
Atglen, PA 19310
Phone: 610-593-1777
Fax: 610-593-2002
Email: info@schifferbooks.com
Web: www.schifferbooks.com

For our complete selection of fine books on this and related subjects, please visit our website at www.betterdaybooks.com. You may also write for a free catalog.

Better Day Books titles are available at special discounts for bulk purchases for sales promotions or premiums. Special editions, including personalized covers, corporate imprints, and excerpts, can be created in large quantities for special needs. For more information, contact the publisher.

felt craft fun

16
Adorable Kawaii-Style Projects to Stitch, Share, and Love All Year Long

Jess DeVos
OTTER BEE STITCHING

BETTER DAY BOOKS®
HAPPY • CREATIVE • CURATED

34

38

44

56

60

66

MUSHROOM
78

82

88

100

104

110

Contents

Welcome!

Everyone has their own embroidery journey—maybe yours is starting today! Mine began in 2017. I was newly separated with two very small children, and I found so much solace in the slow rhythm and repetitive motion of embroidery. As quickly as I fell in love with the craft, I just as quickly realized that spending hours upon hours on satin stitch is not my favorite way to bring color to my work, so I began searching for alternatives.

I didn't know felt appliqué had a name when I started incorporating it into my work, but I did know it was perfect for me. I had experience with making quiet books and other toys, having taught myself to sew when my oldest was a baby, and adding felt into my embroidery felt like bringing that childlike whimsy into a more traditional craft that often gets labeled as stuffy or grandmotherly. While I was a member of a vibrant and growing fiber arts community on social media, it didn't really seem like anyone else was doing what I was doing, and I quickly started creating patterns to share my designs with other makers.

Growing up, I never really saw myself as a creative person. I certainly wasn't an artist. I had friends who were artists, creating photorealistic illustrations in fifth grade, and that definitely wasn't me. At best, I could manage basic cartoon figures. When I began designing felt appliqué patterns, I worried that my drawing skills would hold me back, that people wouldn't be interested in stitching my very simple cartoonish characters. What I didn't realize was that not only is kawaii a very popular art style (and exactly what I was doing), but that if I actually sat down and drew all the time, I would be able to hone my style even more and my skills would improve.

That leads us here to this moment and this book in your hands! I am so excited that you've joined me, and whether I get to introduce you to felt appliqué or you're an experienced stitcher who's just here for the patterns, there is so much joy and whimsy ahead for you. It's an honor to be a resource for your stitching journey, and I hope the skills and techniques you learn in this book give you the confidence to go forward and design your own projects in the future. Ready? Let's get started!

How to Use This Book

This book contains all the information you'll need to work your way through sixteen whimsical projects, each falling into one of three difficulty levels. While the projects can be completed in any order at any time of year, you may wish to use these guidelines when deciding which project to start with.

LEVEL 1: True Beginner Projects

These designs use limited color palettes, simpler shapes, and just a handful of stitches. They are perfect for stitchers who are brand new to the world of embroidery or for experienced stitchers who may be nervous about branching out into working with felt or templates.

LEVEL 2: Adventurous Beginner Projects

These designs use a wider variety of colors and stitches and may have smaller or more-intricate pieces. They're still accessible for true beginners while also allowing you to test and expand your skills if you're a more experienced stitcher.

LEVEL 3: Intermediate Projects

These designs include more-advanced techniques, such as fabric layering or creating illusions through color. They build on skills previously learned in this book so that even new stitchers can complete them.

At the end of each project, you'll also find a few suggestions for adapting the projects to include young stitchers in the process. My kids love to stitch with me, and we often design and complete projects together. I know exactly what parts of the process tend to be more frustration filled than others and have given you my best advice on how to include your children while keeping the project fun and the crafty momentum going. If you have kiddos looking to get involved, I hope you find these sections useful!

Meet Jess

What's your story? What led you to mix felt with embroidery in this particular way?

My first experience with embroidery was a Christmas quiet book I designed for my toddler in 2015. It certainly wasn't a perfect project, but I learned a lot and absolutely loved working with felt as a material. I transitioned to more traditional embroidery in 2017 but was struggling to find enjoyment in hours and hours of satin stitch (and was also really struggling to find my voice as an artist and pattern designer). Remembering that I found a lot of joy in working with felt, I thought, "Why can't I just combine the two?"

When I started making felt appliqué projects, I didn't know that the medium had a name. I didn't see a lot of artists making the kinds of projects I was making and couldn't really find a lot of resources describing the process, so my art process is essentially a giant trial-and-error sequence that is unique to me. I don't necessarily follow all the traditional embroidery rules, but I think my art speaks for itself.

What is your workspace like?

My workspace is the furthest from an Instagram aesthetic! Our home is very small, so I don't really have a designated studio area. I store my materials on a bookshelf tucked away in a corner, I do all my stitching in a very cozy rocking recliner, and I take all my photos on our dining-room table. I would absolutely love to have a peaceful studio space someday, but I'm guessing it's something that will have to wait until my kids are grown (and, honestly, incredible art doesn't need a perfectly curated space to be born in)!

Where do you get inspiration for your designs?

I'm inspired by a lot of things! I love to stitch characters from my favorite shows and movies, and I also find a lot of inspiration in song lyrics I love and books I read. When it comes to designing the bulk of my patterns, I'm inspired by nature and the world around me. I keep a running list of ideas on my phone and always seem to add to it at the strangest times (like when I hop out of the shower or get home from driving somewhere).

I love kawaii-style art, and I think everything looks so much cuter with a little face on it, so nothing is off-limits for me! I've designed animal characters, buildings, plants, food, vehicles, and so much more.

You include tips throughout the book about stitching with kids. When did you and your kids start stitching together, and what was that like?

My kids have always been curious about my work, and my daughter would sit in my lap as a two-year-old and pull the needle up through the fabric as I stitched. It was so much fun sharing that with her (and with my son when he was interested), but it wasn't really something they were super invested in until they were older. In 2020, we were trying to decide on Christmas gifts for family members and landed on making handmade ornaments together. They designed the ornaments and chose the color palettes, and I helped with cutting the pieces and setting them up for stitching. They did the majority of the work, and the ornaments turned out amazingly! It's since become one of our favorite Christmas traditions, and something we make time for every year.

They do both enjoy working on hoop-based projects occasionally, and my daughter is learning to embroider as part of her homeschool curriculum this year (entirely her choice!). I'm hopeful that my younger kids will also get curious as they grow a little older, but, so far, all my three-year-old cares about is making sure each project is thoroughly snuggled when it's complete.

What is one piece of advice you wish you had heard early on in your maker journey?

I wish that someone had told me that it's okay to play when you're creating. I was stuck for a long time in this mentality of following the "rules" and adhering to traditional techniques, but my art and my style really flourished when I gave myself permission to just do what makes me happy. That seems kind of silly, but I think a lot of times when we're learning a new skill, it feels easier to stay within the boundaries of established techniques and advice from skilled instructors. Art doesn't have any rules, and your creativity will really flourish when you break free of those constraints and find the methods and materials that make you happiest.

What do you hope readers will take away from this book?

This book is the resource I didn't have when I started felt appliqué, so I hope it can be that for you. Most of all, I hope you feel empowered to try new things.

I hope this book shows you that beautiful art can come from humble foundations and techniques and that you don't need to be a perfect, experienced maker to create incredible things.

I also hope it inspires you to collaborate with the young makers in your life! Kids are so much fun to work with and have great ideas that sometimes would never even occur to their grown-ups. I can't wait to see what you create!

SALMON
BOYSENBERRY
DMC3803
ALLIUM
DMC3042
SLATE
DMC413
TERRAZZO

1

GETTING STARTED

When we're getting started with a new hobby or craft, sometimes knowing what materials we need or what steps to take can feel overwhelming. Not everyone has an extensive craft stash or the confidence to navigate craft stores without a major case of decision paralysis. Thankfully, I've got you covered! These next few pages will show you exactly what tools and supplies you'll need to invest in to create all the incredible projects in this book. You'll also get my best tips for working with templates, cutting your felt pieces, and getting your hoop prepped perfectly so that stitching is a breeze. Toward the end of the chapter, we'll thoroughly cover embroidery basics, and then we'll cap it all off with an easy sampler for practice. Let's dive in!

Tools and Supplies

As a connoisseur of creative hobbies, my collection of craft supplies is vast. I'm a big believer in buying affordable options when trying out a new hobby and upgrading once you know it's something you want to continue, so I've experimented with a lot of different materials and tools. This section includes not only descriptions of the various tools and supplies you'll need for felt appliqué, but also my recommendations for which options will work best for you based on budget and performance.

Ⓐ Felt

While all the tools and supplies mentioned in this section are important, felt is our top priority. Felt is a soft, textured fabric that won't fray when cut and adds color to appliqué pieces without hours of satin stitch. If you're going to splurge on a single supply, this is the one to splurge on.

There are three main common types of felt. The first is acrylic felt (also known as eco or craft felt). This is the felt you'll find in any big-box craft store. It's made from synthetic fibers that are woven to resemble wool. The other two types are pure wool and wool-blend felt. Both are made from merino wool; wool blend is typically mixed with other fibers such as rayon. I started my journey as an artist using acrylic felt, and you really can make beautiful pieces with it! (I still use acrylic felt to back all my hoops, because it's a lot cheaper to buy in bulk.) Still not sure which felt is right for you? Check out the handy chart below!

I order my project felt exclusively from Benzie Design, a woman-owned craft shop based in Illinois. They carry a huge range of colors (as well as tons of other craft supplies and tools), offer extremely fast shipping, and have excellent customer service. I've been a proud customer since 2018, and you'll find color recommendations from their catalog (listed by name) for each project in this book.

FELT TYPE	Acrylic/Craft/Eco Felt	Wool-Blend Felt	Pure Wool Felt
Pros	• Affordable • Available at most craft stores • Sold in precut sheets	• Nice blend of lower cost and higher quality • Uniform thickness • Very soft and easy to work with • Wide variety of colors	• Uniform thickness • Very soft and easy to work with • Wide variety of colors • Least prone to fraying/pilling (ideal for tiny pieces)
Cons	• More-limited color selection • Doesn't usually have uniform thickness • Prone to stretching, pilling, and tearing • Cannot be ironed (it will melt) • Difficult to mark on without damaging the felt	• May not be available locally • May not be accessible if you have sensitivity to wool	• May not be available locally • May not be accessible if you have sensitivity to wool • Most expensive, so may not work for your budget

Ⓑ Embroidery Floss

Embroidery floss is a bit thicker than typical sewing thread and allows us to adhere felt pieces to the hoop as well as embellish the designs. I exclusively use DMC 6-strand cotton for all my projects. There are other brands, but DMC is widely available in craft stores and fairly affordable, so I've never felt the need to branch out. The strands are soft, the colors won't run if wet, and there are hundreds of colors to choose from (including metallic and glittery options)! I highly recommend shopping name brand for your floss and avoiding any bulk off-brand buys from Amazon, because you won't be able to judge the quality of the floss.

Ⓒ Embroidery Hoops

Embroidery hoops maintain our fabric tension so that our stitching is nice and smooth, and they can also act as the frame for finished pieces. They are available in a wide variety of sizes and materials. When purchasing in craft stores, you'll most commonly find bamboo or plastic hoops. Bamboo can be a decent material to work with, although I've found that often, craft-store embroidery hoops have many gaps between the inner and outer hoops (which will make it impossible to maintain fabric tension), frequent splinters, and subpar hardware that is difficult to tighten. The plastic hoops often maintain tension a bit better but tend to come in bold colors that may clash with your work. There are other online options, such as beechwood hoops from Nurge, wooden hoops from Benzie, or all kinds of hoops from various Etsy suppliers. My personal favorite are Taut Hoops by Stay at Home Artist. They're solid wood, have gorgeous hardware, come in several sizes, are as affordable as craft-store hoops, and you're supporting a small business owner!

Ⓓ Fabric

When I refer to fabric in patterns and written instructions, I'm talking about the base material in the hoop that the design is stitched onto. When choosing a fabric to stitch on, I recommend choosing something with a tight weave (no stretchy knits) that won't be too bulky in your hoop. I exclusively use Robert Kaufman's Kona cotton line of fabrics, largely because they're widely available in my local craft stores and come in a huge variety of colors. Some artists like to use patterned cotton fabrics (selections that come with polka dots, stripes, etc.), but I find that the patterns can distract from the felt design itself. Some prefer the feel of stitching on linen or flannel. Choose what speaks to your heart!

Ⓔ Embroidery Needles

Just like a pencil is your main instrument when drawing, or a crochet hook when crocheting, an embroidery needle is the instrument we use to lay down stitches. They come in different sizes, with 1 being the largest and 12 the smallest. They have a long, oval eye, a long shaft, and a pointed tip, making them perfect for threading several strands of floss and pulling them through fabric with precision. There are numerous brands out there to choose from, but some of my favorites are DMC, John James, and Tulip.

How to choose your perfect needle:

- Eye large enough to thread multiple strands of floss
- Glides through fabric without drag on thread or stress to fabric
- Leaves hole in fabric just wide enough for thread to pass through (size down if the hole is too large)
- My personal favorite is size 3, but you may find a different size works best for you

Ⓕ Scissors

While scissors are important for embroidery in general, they are especially important in appliqué work. We'll be using scissors to cut templates and felt pieces, as well as trimming off floss when we're done stitching. Embroidery scissors come in a variety of shapes and sizes. I own more than eight pairs! When selecting scissors, especially if you're new to embroidery and not looking to spend a lot of money, I recommend choosing a pair that will work for both cutting felt pieces and snipping off embroidery thread. You'll want this pair of scissors to have shorter but sharp blades so that you can cut small detail pieces with ease. I've tried and loved Kai 5000 5.5" (14 cm) detail scissors and Singer ProSeries 4.5" (11.5 cm) detail scissors, but my absolute favorite pair is the Fiskars 5" (12.5 cm) microtip scissors. They maintain their edge so well and make smooth, crisp cuts on any material. The general rule when it comes to craft scissors is to have a designated pair for each material and never use them on anything else, but I use my Fiskars on both paper templates and felt and still get gorgeous edges. I've had the same pair for almost a decade and have never felt the need to switch to anything else!

(G) Writing Utensils

It's sometimes useful to make guidelines or map out the placement of different elements in your projects. My two favorite writing tools for embroidery are chalk pencils and heat-erasable pens.

Chalk pencils can be found at your local fabric store and work best on darker fabric. I use them to transfer designs or figure out the placement of stars, snowflakes, or other small elements when I'm working with a black or dark background. Their main drawback is that the marks can be easily erased or smudged as you work, so you'll want to transfer any designs right before you're ready to stitch (and maybe retrace your lines as you work to avoid losing them entirely).

Heat-erasable pens work for drawing guidelines on lighter fabrics or directly on the felt itself. My favorite pen to use is the Pilot Frixion pen. The guidelines erase with heat (either a hairdryer or iron), but take care, because there can sometimes be a bit of discoloration to your fabric or felt if you don't stitch directly on top of a line. (I've found that it can sometimes be removed by dabbing with a damp paper towel, and it seems that some colors don't have the issue at all.)

(H) Hot-Glue Gun

Hot glue is an excellent adhesive for closing hoops. The glue gun allows for precise application, which makes adhering fabric to the slim edge of your embroidery hoop a breeze. I don't have any specific brand preference, and you can buy the cheapest option available. You'll want a mini glue gun with low heat to minimize any burns that could occur from touching the hot glue as you manipulate your hoop. Remember that hot glue cools and hardens very quickly, which can be either a blessing or a curse depending on the situation.

(I) Straight Pins

Straight pins make it easy to keep felt pieces in the correct place while stitching. They can be found in the sewing section of any craft store, and there's no need to splurge for quality. They often come in a small case with plenty of pins for multiple projects. Get the type with a ball on one end so they don't get lost in your projects.

Working with Templates

When it comes to traditional embroidery patterns, the entire design is transferred to your fabric before you begin stitching so that you have guidelines to work with. With felt appliqué patterns, it's more like a puzzle than a coloring sheet, and we'll be building our design out of various felt shapes. Each design in this book comes with coordinating templates at the back of that book that are perforated for easy removal. I recommend photocopying and storing templates in envelopes or small baggies to keep them together and for future reuse. Let's look at a few different ways to transfer those shapes to your felt!

A note on template sizes: Some of the template pieces in this book's projects are really small, to the point that they may feel intimidating to cut out. I promise that everything is manageable with patience and care (and the freezer paper method described here is often the easiest method for those teeny-tiny pieces). If, however, you're finding that it's just not working for you, those tiny details can always be drawn on with a heat-erasable pen and embroidered!

Method 1: Pin and Cut

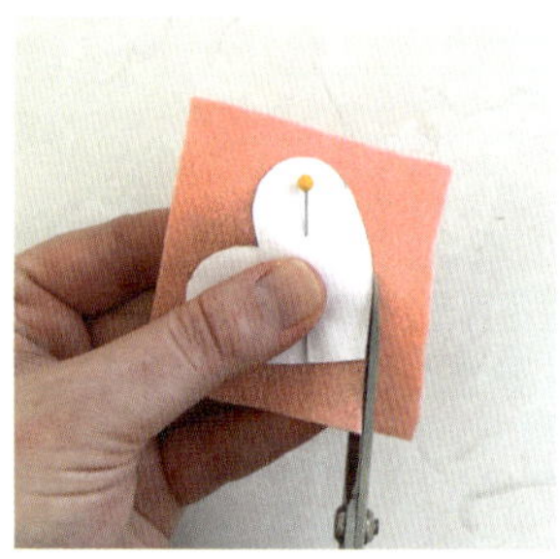

The quickest option for cutting out templates is to pin the template to the felt with straight pins and cut around the outside of the shape. However, this is not my preferred method. Pinning only works for pieces that are large enough for pins to fit, so tiny pieces will have to be held in place by hand as you work. Without having the template perfectly flush and secured to the felt, there is a chance your template could shift, which will make your felt piece the wrong size or shape. You'll also be puncturing your templates, which could make them unusable over time. (You can solve this by photocopying the template pages in this book and pinning the photocopies.) While this method can work in a pinch, we've got better options available!

Method 2: Trace and Cut

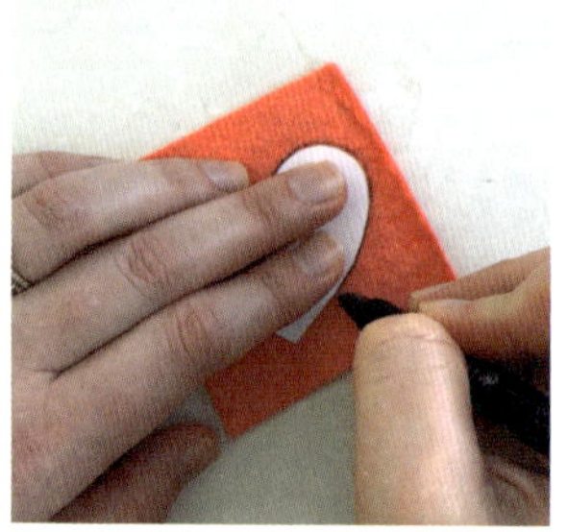

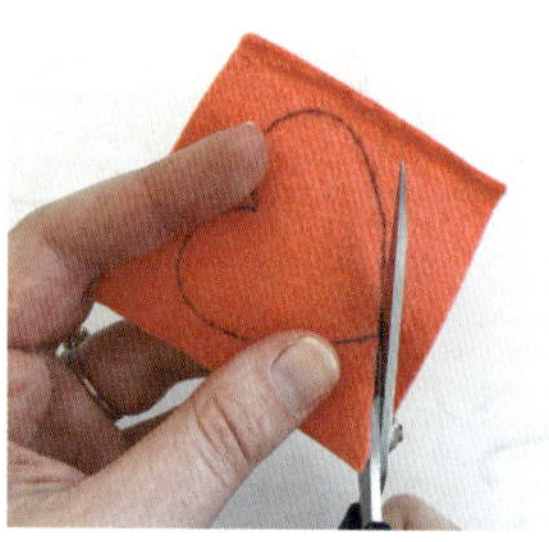

For lighter shades of felt, use a heat-erasable pen to trace the shape onto the felt. Hold the paper template in place with your nondominant hand and use your dominant hand to trace. If using this method, you may wish to photocopy your templates onto cardstock or transfer the templates to a thin cardboard (like the material of a cereal box). This will make your templates sturdier and less prone to slipping when tracing. When drawing on felt, use small strokes (almost like sketching motions) to avoid pulling or tearing the fibers. Once the shape is completely traced, you can cut it out with your scissors. A heat source (hairdryer or small iron) will erase any pen markings that are still visible after cutting.

Method 3: Freezer Paper

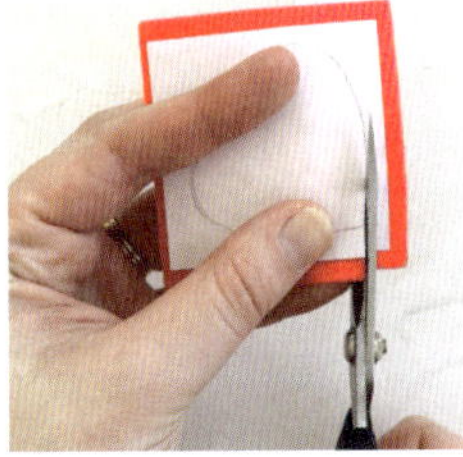

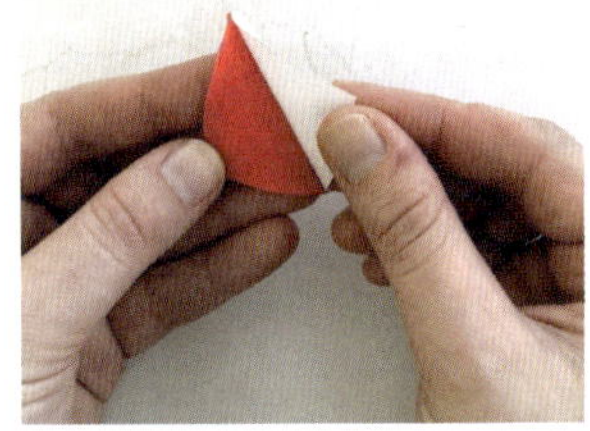

For darker shades of felt that won't show pen marks, or if you want to be sure the pattern pieces won't shift at all, freezer paper is an excellent option. To begin, trace your template with a pencil onto the dull side of the freezer paper. Next, place your template shiny side down on top of your felt, and iron in place. Use scissors to cut out the template, then simply peel the freezer paper away! This option won't work as well if you're using acrylic felt, as that material doesn't always hold up well to ironing.

Tips for smooth cuts:

- **Be sure your scissors are sharp!** Dull scissors will tug at the fibers, tearing them rather than gliding through. The best way to keep your scissors sharp is to designate a pair for paper and a pair for felt (though the Fiskars pair I mention on page 17 has never had an issue alternating between those two materials).
- **Rotate the felt while cutting, not the scissors.** The wrist holding your scissors should be straight most of the time. By rotating the felt piece with your nondominant hand, your cuts will be smooth rather than jagged.
- **For sharp corners, make precise snips with the tip of the scissors.** This will keep corners extra crisp and eliminate wisps of fabric in tight spaces.
- **Begin your cuts a millimeter or two before you need to.** This tip is perhaps the hardest to explain without a demonstration. Suppose you're cutting a circle. Your scissors are nearly closed, and you're ready to start a new cutting motion while maintaining a smooth curve. Rather than beginning your new cut exactly where the previous one ended, line your scissors up so that the new cut will begin just slightly before the previous one ended. Not only does this allow you to be in position and rotating your felt before your scissors begin cutting, but it will also trim off any slight sharp edges, keeping your lines smooth and curved as intended.

Prepping Your Hoop

Getting your hoop ready for stitching is a crucial part of the embroidery process. If this is your very first experience with embroidery, we want it to be fun so that you feel encouraged to try other projects, and having loose fabric that won't maintain its tension is a quick way to make embroidery feel frustrating. Let's look at the best way to get your hoop all ready to go! You'll want to work on a sturdy, flat surface, like a table or desk, and don't worry about ironing your fabric first (unless you just want to or have particularly deep creases in your fabric). If your fabric tension is correct, you won't see any wrinkles!

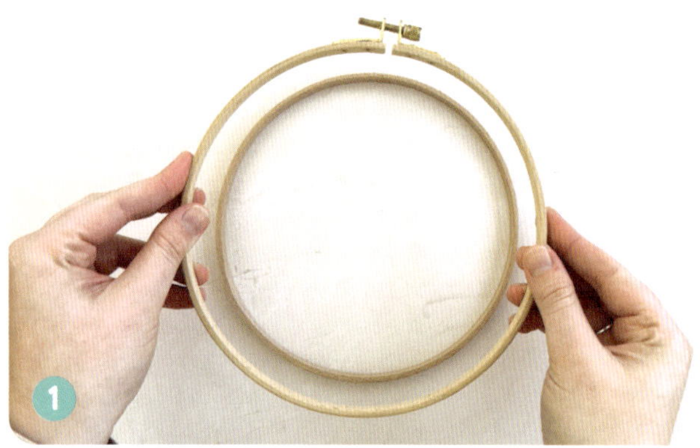

1. Separate the inner and outer hoops. Unscrew the hardware at the top of the hoop so that tension is released. Remove the outer hoop and set it aside.

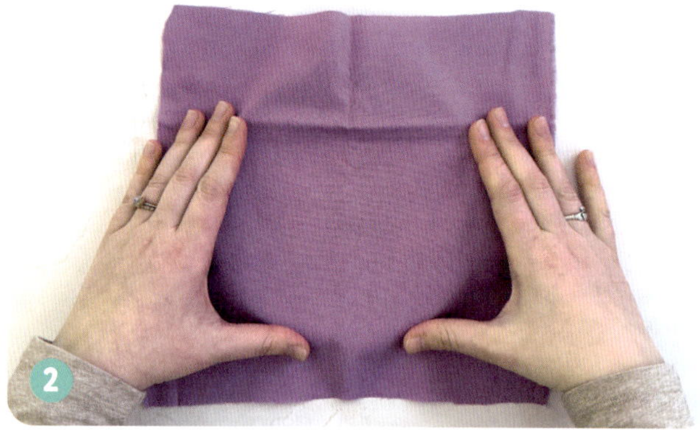

2. Prepare your fabric. Cut a piece of fabric that measures 2" (5 cm) wider than your hoop width (for example, if you're working with an 8" [20 cm] hoop, cut a 10" x 10" [25 x 25 cm] square of fabric). Position your fabric over the inner hoop. Be sure your fabric is centered over the smaller inner ring, so that you have an even amount of fabric—about 1" (2.5 cm) of overhang—on all sides.

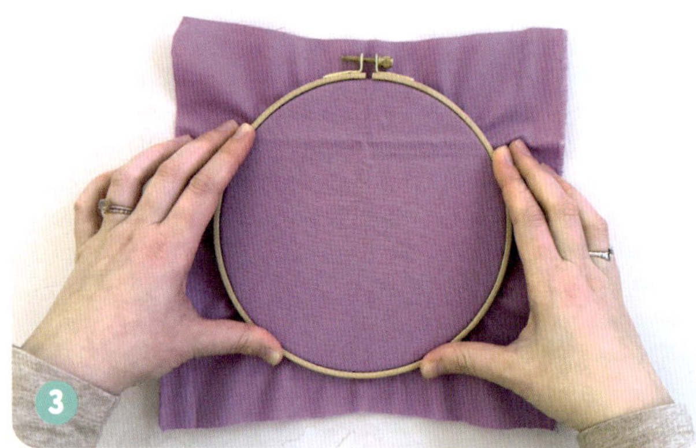

3. Place the outer hoop. Position the outer hoop over the fabric and the inner hoop, making sure your hardware is at the top, and gently press down until both hoops are resting on your flat surface.

4. Tighten the hardware. Using your nondominant hand, gently pull the top edge of the fabric down and away from the hoop so that it's smooth and flat inside the hoop. With your dominant hand, tighten the hardware a few turns (but not all the way just yet).

Tip:
Depending on what type of hoop you're using, you may need to use a screwdriver to fully tighten your hardware!

5. Pull the fabric taut. Moving in a circle, gently pull the fabric so that it's nice and smooth inside your hoop. Give the hardware another few turns to tighten once you've made it all the way around. We want our fabric to be "drum tight," meaning if you tap on the surface of your fabric, it feels firm under your finger and sounds a bit like a drum. Continue pulling your fabric gently and tightening the hardware until everything is nice and secure.

6

6. Trim your fabric. Trim your fabric in a circle, leaving about ½"–¾" (1.3–2 cm) of overhang. Doing this now makes it less likely that you'll end up stitching through the excess as you work, which means less frustration as you're stitching!

You did it! Your hoop is all prepped and ready for stitching. Having a solid foundation to stitch on is an important piece of creating beautiful works of fiber art, so congratulations on a successful first step!

Embroidery Basics

Now that we've gotten your materials ready, and prepped your templates and your hoop, let's jump in with some basic skills you'll need for embroidery. The next few pages will teach you how to get your floss and needle ready for stitching, as well as give you the skills and confidence to start, stop, and execute several beginner stitches. Don't let the "beginner" designation fool you into thinking you'll be creating basic or boring designs, though. These foundational skills will have you creating incredible pieces of art in no time!

Basic Skills

Separating 6-Strand Floss

Let's start by learning how to separate strands of floss. Skeins of DMC 6-strand cotton floss (and most other brands of standard embroidery floss) consist of six individual strands of thread bundled together into one thicker thread. For felt appliqué, we will rarely work with more than three strands at once, so being able to separate strands without frustration is key.

1. **Cut a length of floss about 30" (76 cm) long.** This measurement does not have to be exact! My favorite way to measure the length to cut is to hold the end of the floss in my right hand and extend it to the center of my chest. This is a perfect length to work with (and may not be exactly 30"/ 76 cm for you).

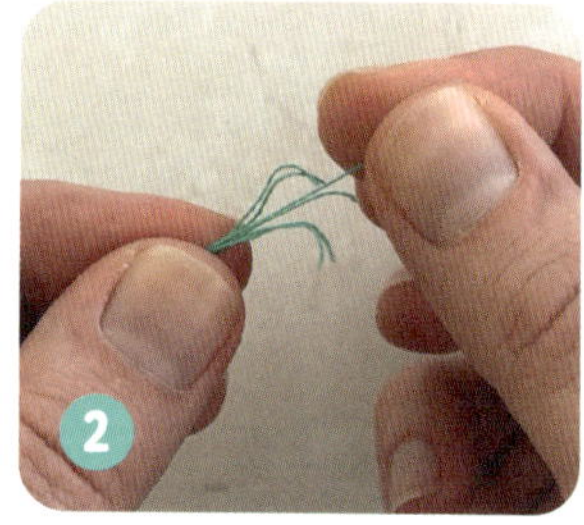

2. **Grab an individual strand.** Hold the floss near one end with your nondominant hand and find an individual strand with your dominant hand.

3. **Separate the strand.** Gently pull that single strand while keeping a firm but gentle grip on the remaining floss. The single strand should just slip free. If you need more than one strand, repeat this process for each strand needed, then group them together to thread your needle.

Threading Your Needle

Getting your floss threaded is a crucial step to begin embroidering, and it can often feel intimidating to new stitchers. But it doesn't have to be daunting! Half of the success of threading your needle comes from choosing the right needle (refer to page 16). The other half is having a confident guide walk you through the process, which is where I come in.

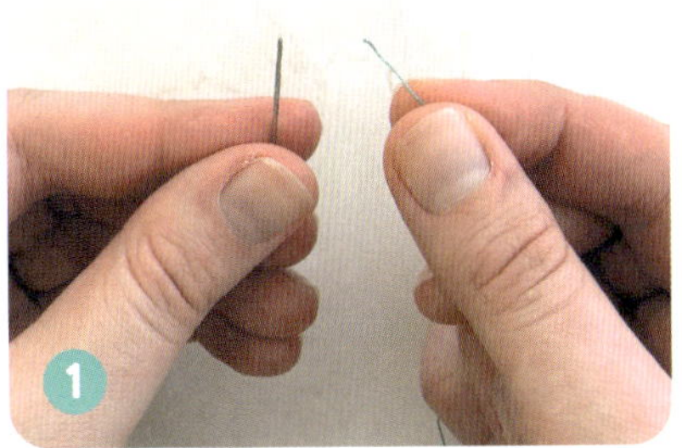

1. Grip your needle and your floss. Hold your needle just below the eye with your nondominant hand. Hold your floss in your dominant hand about ½" (1.3 cm) from one end.

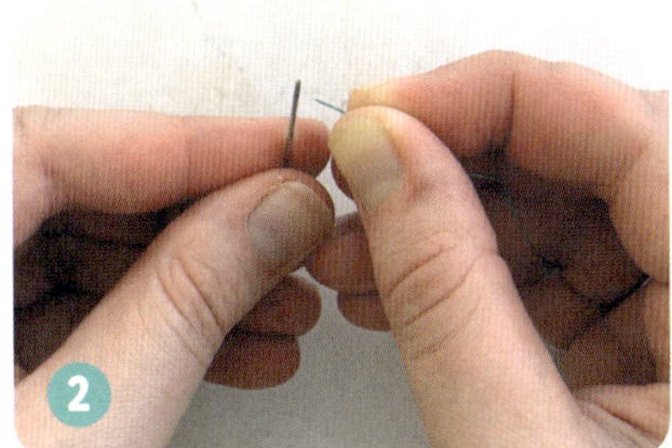

2. Prepare your floss. Dampen the end of your floss lightly using your own saliva. This will get all the fibers smoothed together (even if you only have one strand of floss) and make it easy for the thread to glide straight through the eye of your needle.

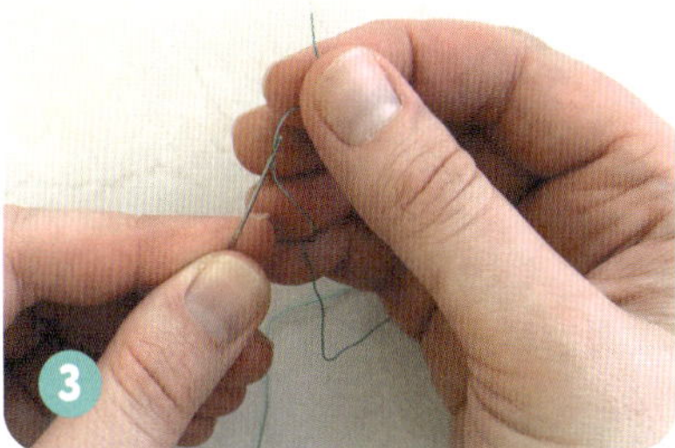

3. Thread the needle. Guide the floss through the eye of the needle and pull the floss the rest of the way through. It's okay if you need to hold it close to your face or go slowly to make sure things are aligning the way they need to.

If you find this process difficult, you can try using a needle threader, which are widely available in big-box craft stores. Their only drawback is that they may not fit through the eye of your needle if the eye is on the smaller side. You'll need to be sure that the threader you purchase will fit the size of the needle you're using. Here's how use a needle threader.

1. Insert the needle threader. Put the hooked end of the needle threader through the eye of your needle.

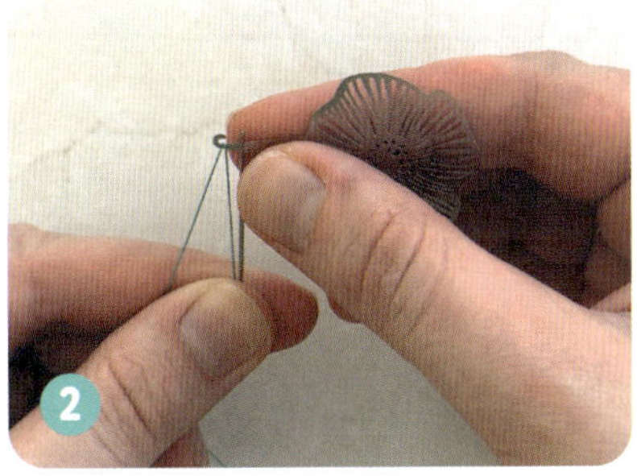

2. Drape your floss over the hook. Place your floss over the hooked end of the needle threader, making sure that there's at least 1" (2.5 cm) or so of overhang (we don't want the floss slipping off the hook).

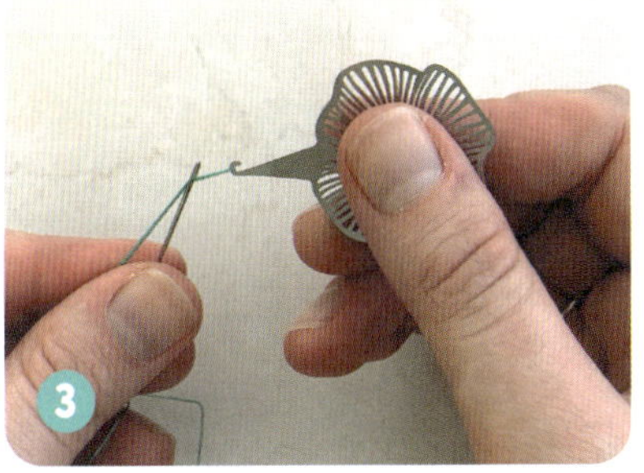

3. Pull the hook and floss back through the eye of your needle. Slowly bring the hook back through the eye of the needle, making sure the floss comes with it. Remove the threader and continue pulling the floss all the way through so that you have several inches of thread tail.

Starting Your Stitching

There are two schools of thought when it comes to threaded floss: You either knot one end of the floss and leave a long thread tail as you stitch, or you double your floss over and knot both ends together. I don't like the idea of possibly losing my needle or the end of my thread between layers of felt if it comes unthreaded as I work, so, for the projects in this book, we'll be doubling it over. I especially recommend the doubled-over method for younger stitchers. Here's how to begin stitching.

Tip:

If you prefer to work with a thread tail instead of the doubling-over method, make sure to double all the thread counts found in the project instructions.

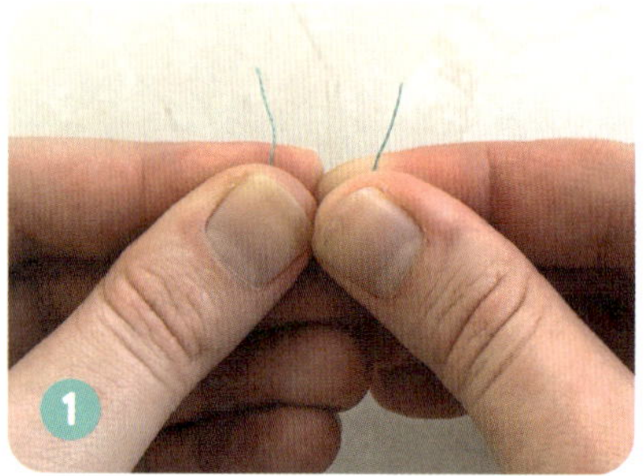

1. Bring both ends of your floss together. Grab an end in each hand and bring the ends together. Let your needle dangle freely.

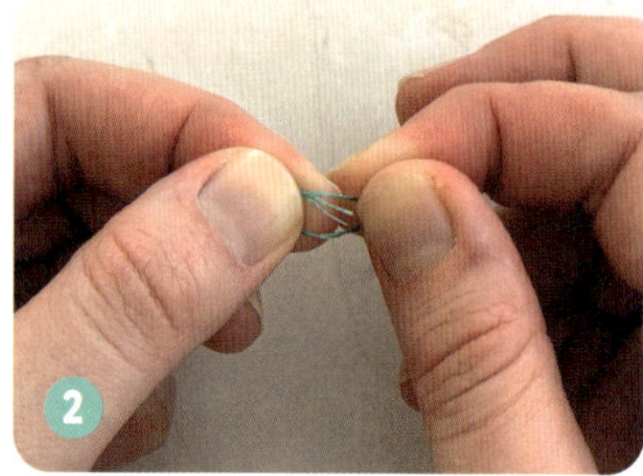

2. Make a knot at the end. Wrap the floss around your nondominant index finger and push the tail through the loop you've created. Tighten slowly as you move the knot toward the end of the floss. Repeat this step two to three times for a secure knot.

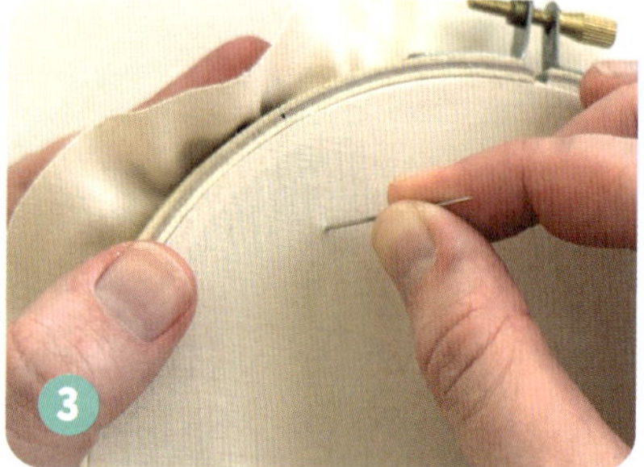

3. Bring your needle up at your beginning point. Once your thread is knotted, bring your needle to the center of the thread loop and begin stitching!

Stopping Your Stitching

Finished with the section you're working on? Running out of floss and need to tie off so you can rethread your needle? Let's look at how to stop stitching. You'll want to tie off when you have 2"–3" (5–7.5 cm) of unused floss, to make sure you have enough slack to easily secure your stitching.

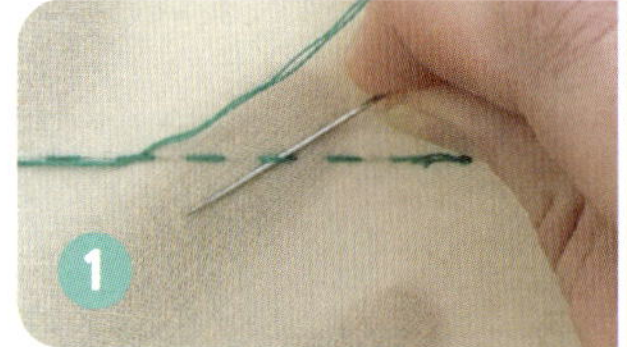

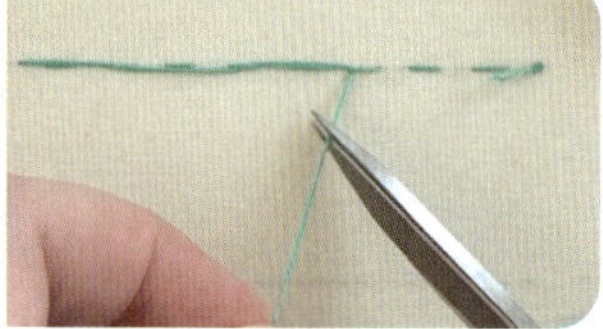

Option 1: Turn your hoop over and run your needle under a few stitches. Trim the floss so that a small tail is sticking out of the final stitch. I prefer to use this method most often because it's fast and requires minimal effort.

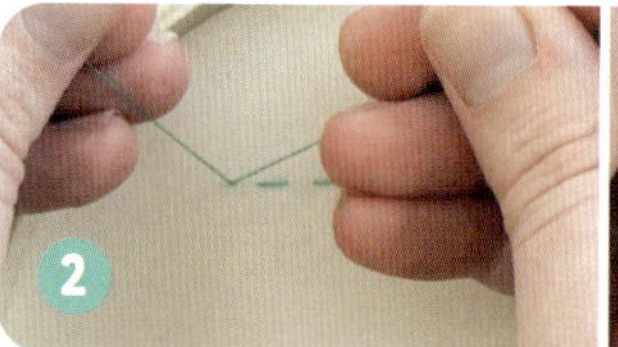

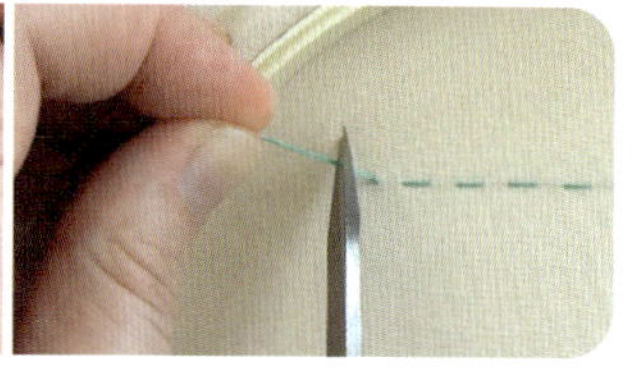

Option 2: If the end of your stitching isn't near any other stitches (when you're making French knots across a wide area, for example), or if you just feel more comfortable with knotted floss, you can tie off the floss. Turn your hoop over and trim the floss near the eye of your needle, leaving long tails. Separate the tails into two sides and tie a knot. Repeat two to three times to make sure your knot is nice and secure, then trim the tails down.

Dealing with Knots

Unfortunately, knots are an inevitable part of stitching. Here are tips for how to prevent knots and what to do if you encounter a knot.

Use thread gloss/conditioner: This will help your floss glide smoothly through your fabric without tangling. Use just a very thin layer to avoid a lot of buildup on the surface of the felt.

Let your thread dangle occasionally: As you're stitching, your floss will begin twisting as a result of the motion, making it more prone to tangling up. Periodically, as you're stitching, simply let your needle dangle (from the backside of your hoop is easiest). The floss will gently untwist in a matter of seconds, and you can get back to stitching.

Keep calm: If you see the thread beginning to tangle up on itself as you work, stop and untangle it before continuing to pull your floss through.

Use your needle to loosen the threads: Avoid pulling your floss too tightly in any direction if you see a knot. Most knots can be easily untangled by using your needle to loosen the strands (it more easily gets between the strands than your fingers can).

Trim and tie off floss: If you have a pesky knot that's not coming undone, trim your floss just below the knot and tie it off on the back. You may need to unpick a few stitches to get enough length to tie off. Once that's done, rethread your needle and keep going!

Basic Stitches

One of my favorite things about felt appliqué is that you can create stunning pieces of art with only a few basic stitches in your tool belt. The following nine stitches will be used often throughout this book and are some of the easiest to learn if you're new to the world of embroidery. Let's take a look!

Running Stitch

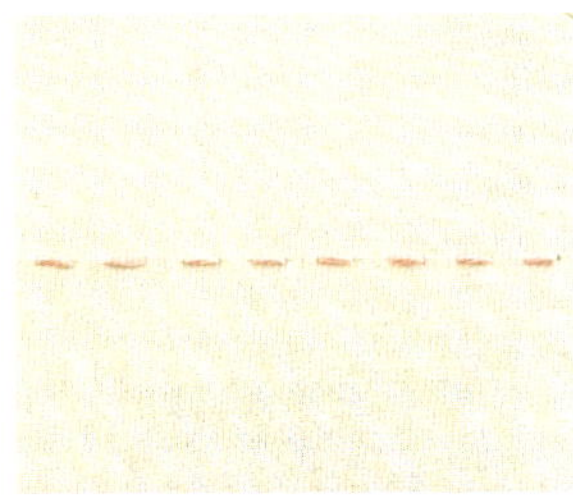

This is the main stitch we'll be using for every single project. Luckily, it's also incredibly easy!

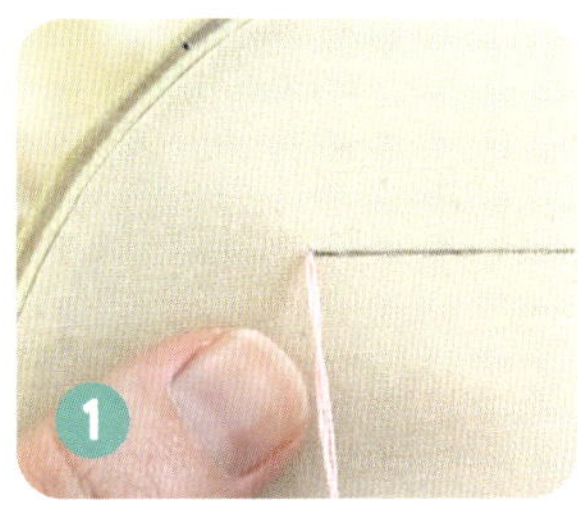

1. Begin your first stitch. Bring your needle up at point A.

2. Complete your stitch. Bring your needle back down at point B. That's one stitch!

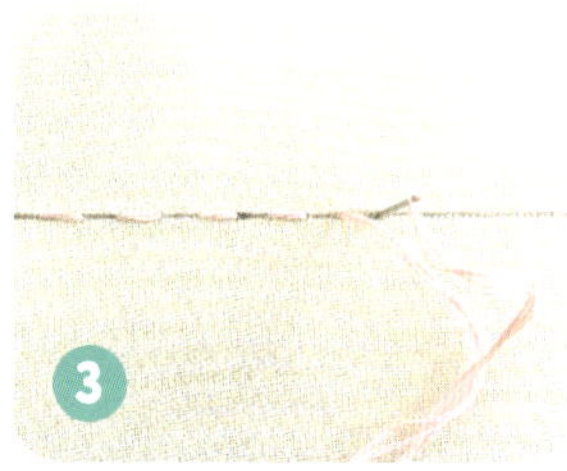

3. Repeat until complete. Move about one stitch length away, come up from the bottom at point C, and bring your needle back down at point D. Repeat until you complete the line or shape.

Backstitch

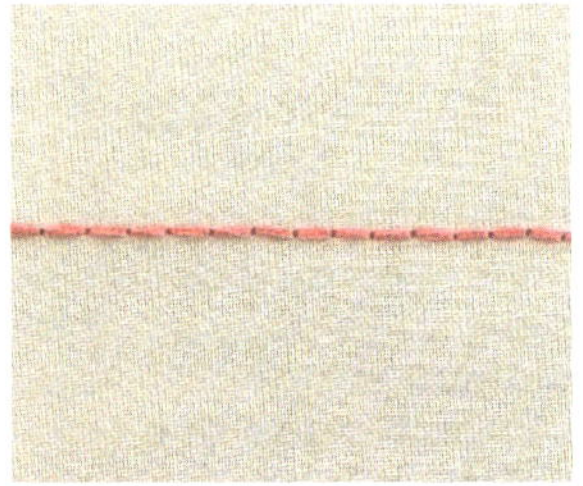

While running stitch creates a dashed-line effect, backstitch is best for creating a smooth line.

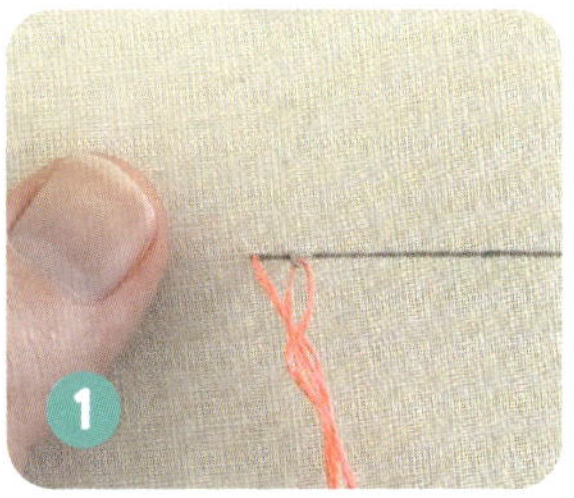

1. Begin with a single stitch. Just like you would with a running stitch, bring your needle up at point A and back down at point B. This is one stitch.

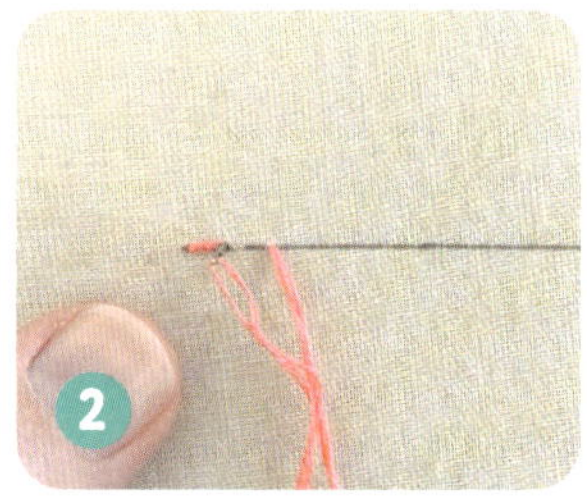

2. Continue your backstitch. Bring your needle up at point C and back down at point B. With backstitch, we're working "backward" to create a smooth line of stitches.

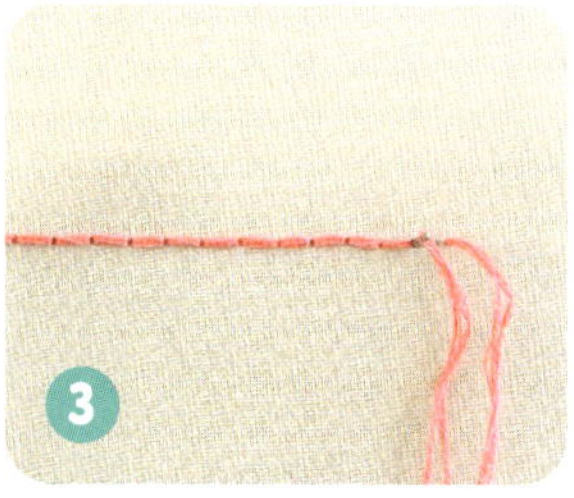

3. Repeat until complete. Continue stitching by bringing your needle up about one stitch length away and back down through the same hole as your previous stitch. Aim for a short and uniform stitch length on curves to keep them smooth!

Whipped Backstitch

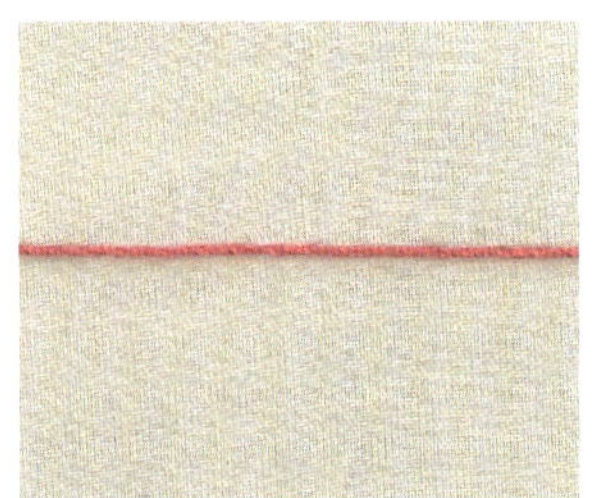

This stitch smooths out your backstitch even more, creating the appearance of a seamless line.

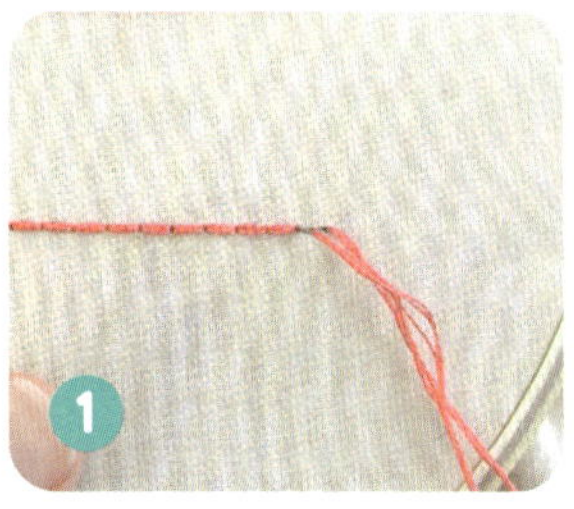

1. Complete your backstitch as normal. Refer to the instructions for backstitch if needed.

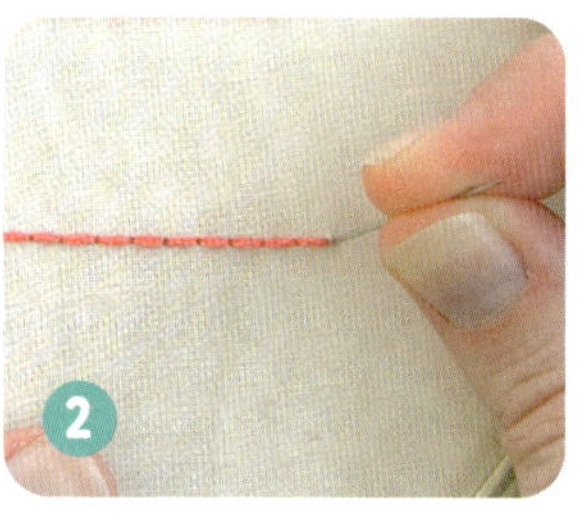

2. Change threads. Thread your needle with the thread you'll be using to whip. This can be the same as your backstitch thread (for a seamless look) or different (for a striped effect). Use the same number of strands as you did for your backstitch. If you have enough floss left after your backstitch, you can just continue with the same thread!

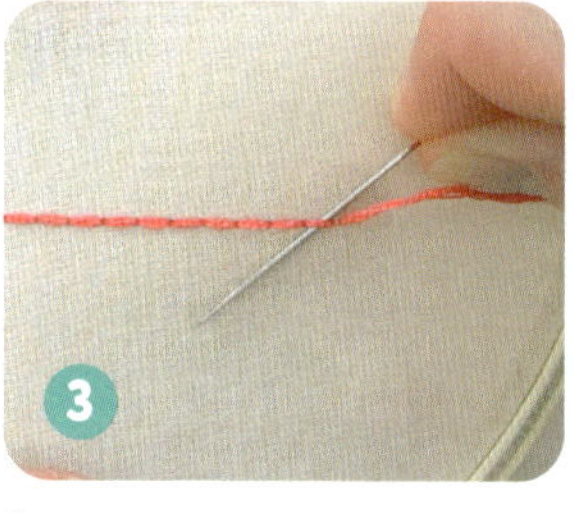

3. Whip your backstitch. Bring your needle up right next to your first backstitch and slide the needle under the stitch. Repeat along the length of the entire line of shape, making sure to bring your needle under the stitches from the same side every time. I like to whip from right to left.

Tip:

This stitch can be difficult to execute on felt, since it's nearly impossible to avoid grabbing felt fibers as you whip (which will make your floss look fuzzy rather than smooth and seamless). It will work best if done on your background fabric, if possible.

Chain Stitch

Chain stitch is a series of interlocking stitches that create the appearance of a chain. It's useful for adding light strings, banners, or other pretty details.

1. **Begin your chain.** Bring your needle up at point A and back down at the same point. Pull your floss most of the way through, leaving a 1" (2.5 cm) loop.

2. **Anchor the loop.** Bring your needle up at point B, making sure that your needle point is coming up through the loop. Maintain gentle tension in your floss as you pull the stitch taut. You've created your first chain!

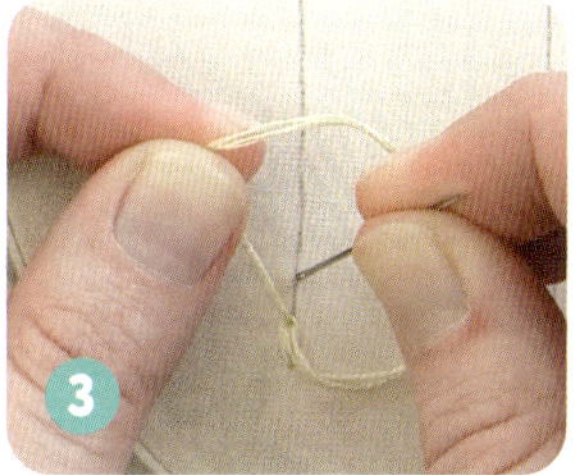

3. **Continue stitching until complete.** Repeat steps 1 and 2 until you've finished the section you're stitching or run out of floss. To tie off, create an anchor stitch by bringing your needle down just to the outside of your final thread loop.

Tip:

If you run out of floss before the end of your chain, anchor it like normal and rethread your needle. When it's time to rejoin, bring your needle up through the anchor stitch inside your last loop and resume stitching.

Detached Chain Stitch

Detached chain stitch, also known as a lazy daisy, is excellent for creating flower petals or leaves.

1. **Create one chain.** Bring your needle up at point A and back down at the same point. Pull your floss most of the way through, leaving a 1" (2.5 cm) loop.

2. **Anchor the loop.** Bring your needle up at point B, making sure that your needle point is coming up through the loop. Maintain gentle tension in your floss as you pull the stitch taut. Bring your needle back down just outside your floss loop to anchor the chain.

3. **Repeat as needed.** Create individual leaves or flower petals with as many detached chains as you like!

Fly Stitch

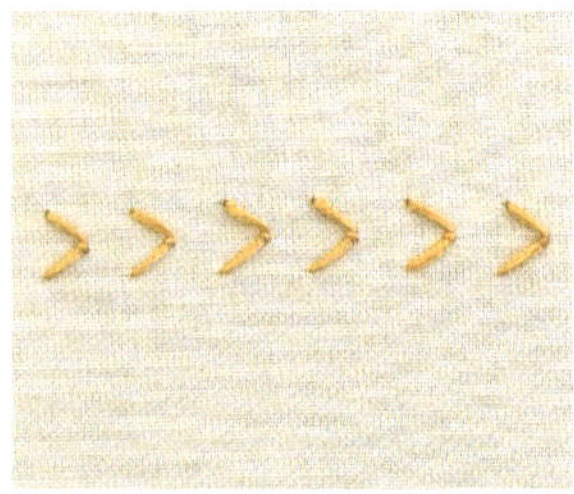

A fly stitch is a stitch in a "V" shape instead of a loop or straight line. It works well for adding scale texture to animals, sprout shapes to garden scenes, or even basic mouths to kawaii-style faces.

1. Begin your fly stitch. Bring your needle up at point A and down at point B. Don't pull your floss all the way through immediately—leave a 1" (2.5 cm) loop.

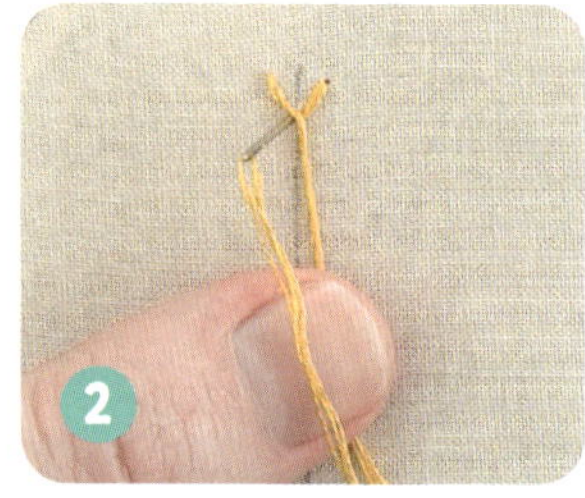

2. Create your anchor stitch. Bring your needle up at point C (a few millimeters down from your original stitch and centered between the ends) and pull your floss taut. Bring your needle back down at point D, just to the opposite side of the floss, to create an anchor stitch.

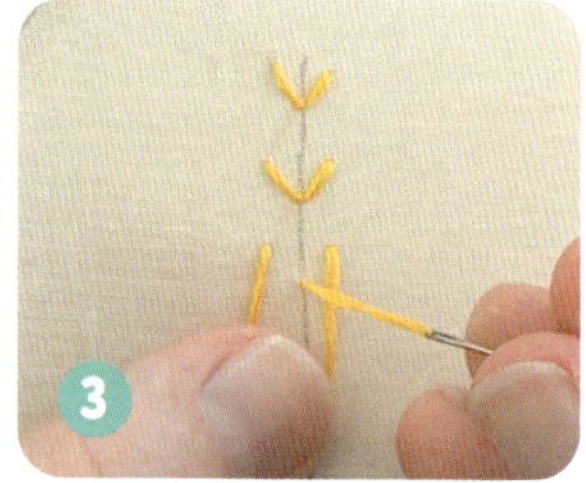

3. Repeat as needed. Make as many fly stitches as needed for the desired effect!

French Knot

The key to successful French knots is tension. You'll need both hands free, so you may want to work with your hoop on a table (other options include putting a pillow in your lap or using a hoop stand).

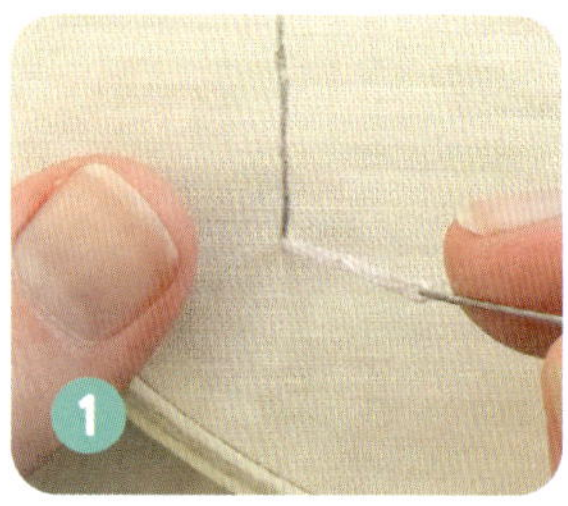

1. Begin your knot. Bring your needle up at point A.

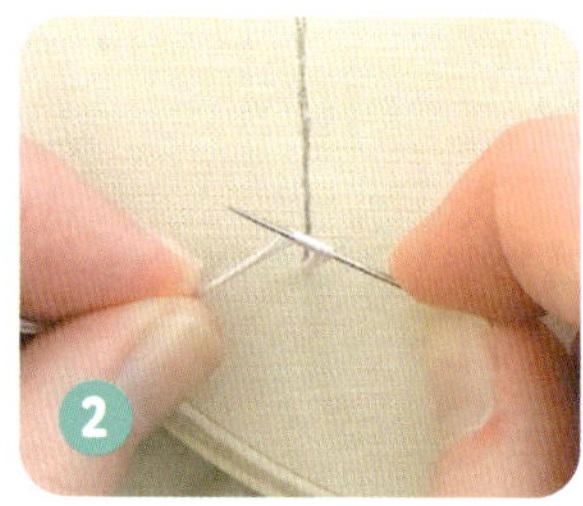

2. Wrap your floss. Wrap your floss around the needle twice. (You can experiment with size by using more or fewer strands of floss or wrapping the floss more or fewer times around the needle.)

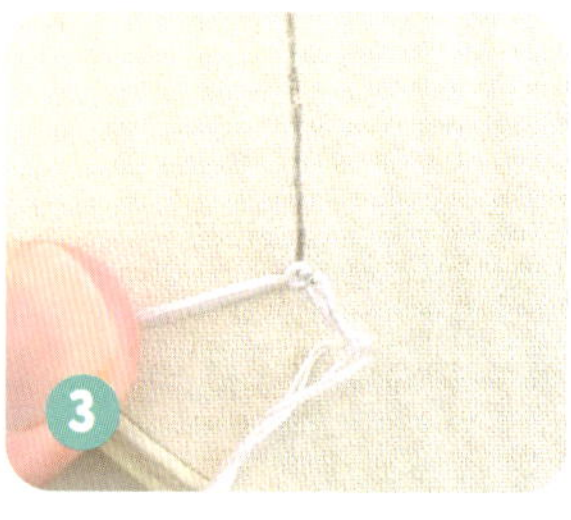

3. Complete your knot. Bring your needle back down slightly to the side of point A. Be sure to maintain the tension in your nondominant hand as you pull your needle all the way through with your dominant hand. You can release the floss when you have 1"–2" (2.5–5 cm) left to pull through.

Fill Stitch

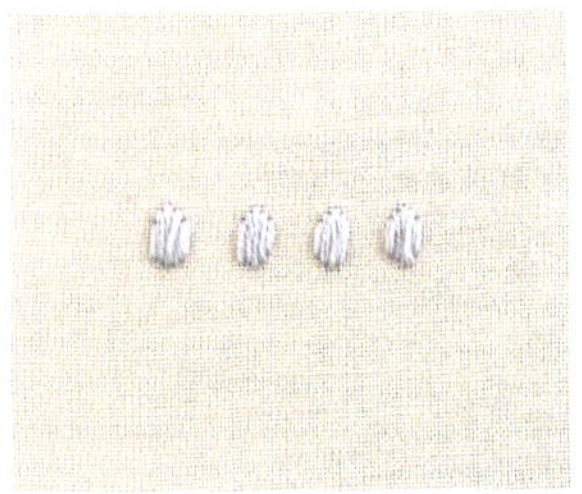

Fill stitches are essentially satin stitches, but in a tiny area. We'll be using this stitch to fill in eyes and cheeks for some of our characters.

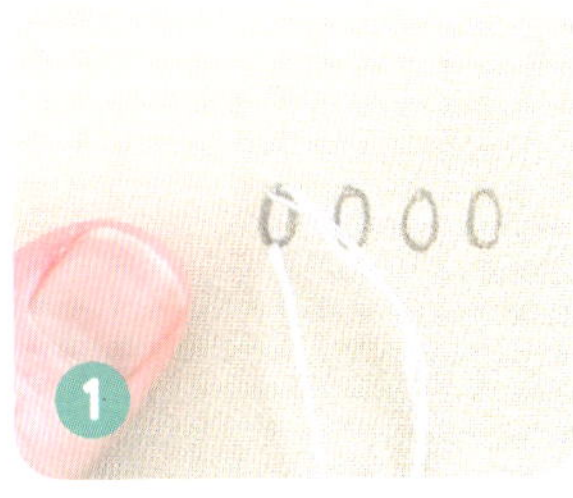

1. **Make a single vertical stitch in the center.** Bring your needle up at the very bottom of your oval and back down at the very top of your oval. This will be the longest stitch we make in this area. (Note: if you're filling in cheeks, work horizontally instead.)

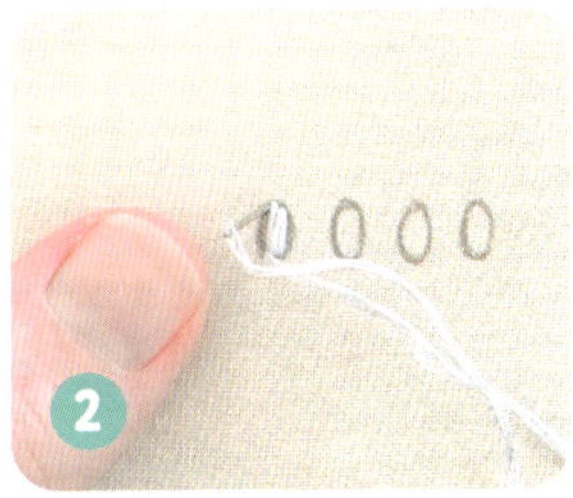

2. **Add a stitch to either side.** Now make a slightly shorter stitch on each side of the center stitch. Decreasing our stitch length as we work outward will create the impression of a curve and make the eye or cheek look rounded.

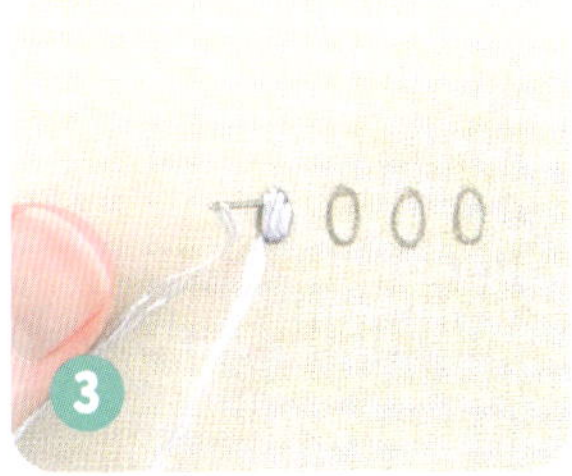

3. **Repeat until complete.** Continue adding stitches to fill the desired shape. It typically only takes two to three stitches on each side of the center to make a nicely shaped oval for an eye or cheek. If you don't feel like your curves look smooth, you can also backstitch around the outside of your oval.

Couching Stitch

Couching stitches hold felt in place without actually stitching into the felt itself.

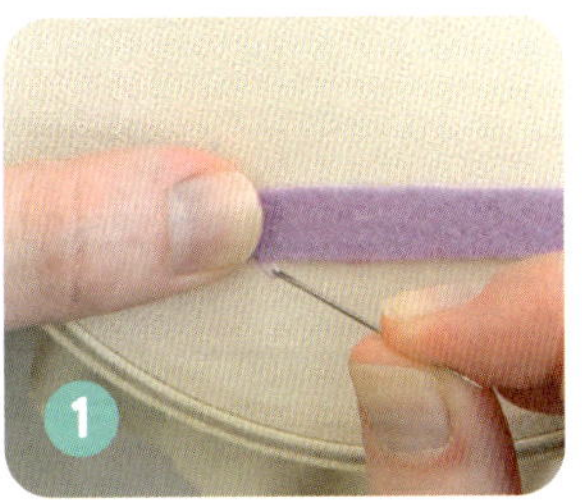

1. **Begin your stitch.** Bring your needle up at point A, just outside the edge of your felt piece.

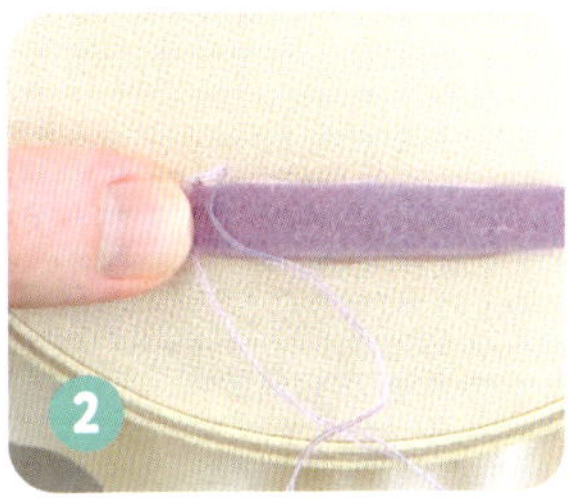

2. **Complete your stitch.** Bring your needle back down at point B, just outside of the opposite edge of your felt piece. You may wish to make the ends of your stitch directly across from each other or at an angle, depending on the desired effect.

3. **Repeat as needed.** Continue making couching stitches as many times as necessary to secure the piece. To conserve floss, begin your next stitch on the same side that you ended your previous stitch on.

Shooting-Star Sampler

Now that you have all the basic skills and stitch knowledge that you need, let's dip our toes in the felt appliqué pool with a little sampler project. This is a great way to make sure you've got a good handle on all the techniques you'll need to create the projects in this book. This little shooting star brings some rainbow cheer to your space and gives you the opportunity to practice everything you've learned! Especially if you're working with young stitchers, this is a great place to start building some serious crafting confidence.

I used felt from Benzie Design in the color parchment and DMC floss in colors black, gray, pink, orange, yellow, green, and blue to complete this project in an 8" (20 cm) hoop. However, there are so many color palettes that would be fun for this design, so feel free to customize it to suit your space and aesthetic!

Templates on page 133.

Backstitch
Whipped backstitch
French knot
Chain stitch
Detached chain stitch
Running stitch
Fill stitch
Couching stitch
Fly stitch

2

PROJECTS

We've made it! At this point, you have all the basic knowledge and skills to be able to jump in and start stitching. The following pages contain all the materials, stitches, and instructions you'll need to complete any of the sixteen different projects. Designing this collection stretched my creative muscles in entirely new ways, and bringing these pieces to life brought me immense joy. Even for someone with years of experience, there's nothing quite like seeing all those felt layers and stitches come together into one incredible piece of art. I hope you enjoy these projects as much as I did. Let's get started!

make a wish

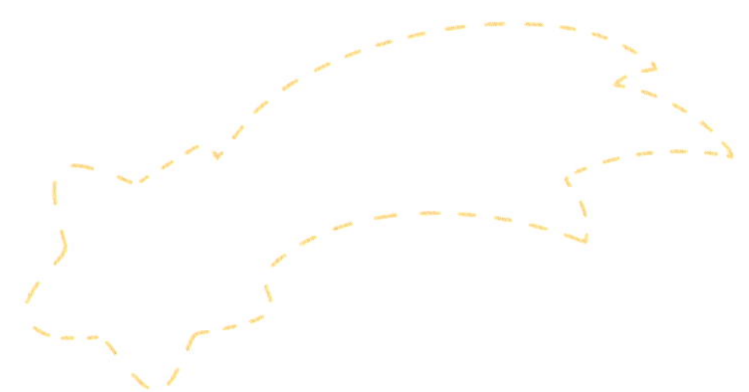

I don't know about you, but I am absolutely a "look at the moon" person. Full moons especially are so ethereal and beautiful; they never fail to fill me with a sense of wonder and awe. That beauty may be a reason why full moons are one of my favorite things to stitch in felt. The shapes are simple and easy to work with for even the newest stitchers, but you can create so much character and depth with the most-basic components! I never place my craters in the same way twice, which means each moon is a one-of-a-kind creation. This makes a happy little moon the perfect place to start our embroidery journey.

This design uses a handful of the most-basic stitches and a simple color palette to create a breathtaking starry scene with plenty of room for customization.

Templates on page 134.

supplies

- 8" (20 cm) embroidery hoop
- cotton fabric in black
- felt in colors shown at right
- 6-strand embroidery floss in colors: light yellow, dark yellow, light gray, medium gray, dark gray, black, pink
- white felt for backing

tools

- embroidery needle
- straight pins
- scissors
- heat-erasable pen
- chalk pencil
- hot-glue gun

stitches used

- running stitch
- backstitch
- French knot

felt colors

parchment

 silver

 smoke

canary

custard

black

pink

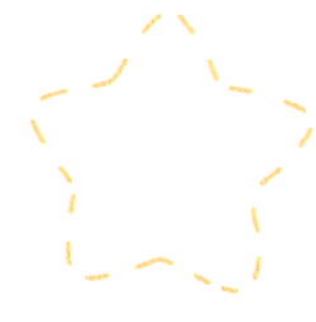

make a wish

1. Stitch the shooting-star base. Pin the shooting star and moon base layers to your fabric. Using one strand of light-yellow floss, make a running stitch around the outer edge of the shooting star.

2. Embellish the shooting star. Position the star shape on top of the base layer. Hold in place with your thumb as you make a running stitch along the outer edge using one strand of dark-yellow floss. Use a heat-erasable pen to draw two curved lines on the tail. Backstitch both lines using one strand of dark-yellow floss.

3. Stitch the moon base layer. Now that the star is complete, let's move on to stitching the moon. Using one strand of light-gray floss, make a running stitch around the outer edge of the base layer.

4. Add craters to the moon. Position your crater pieces on the surface of the moon. Use one strand of coordinating floss (medium gray or dark gray) to make a running stitch around each crater.

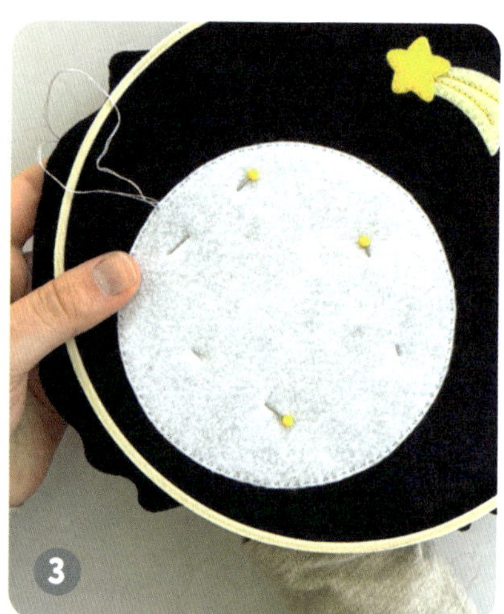

Because these pieces are too small to pin, you'll want to work slowly and carefully so as not to shift them around. Alternatively, remove any pieces you're not actively stitching and reposition them later.

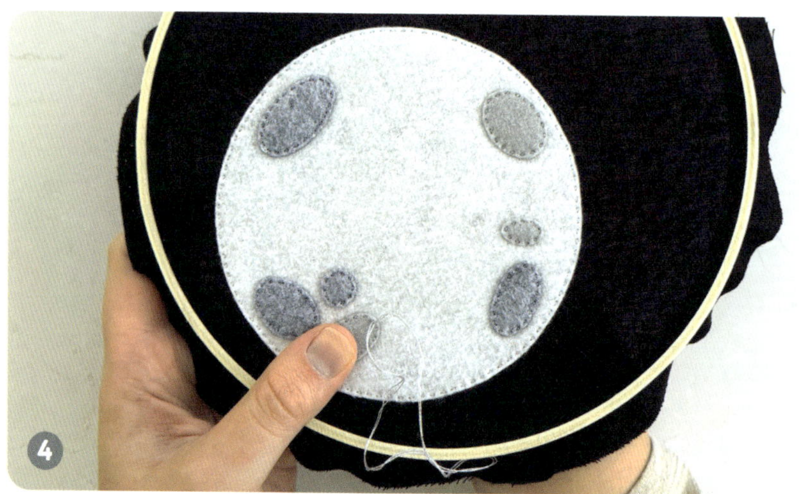

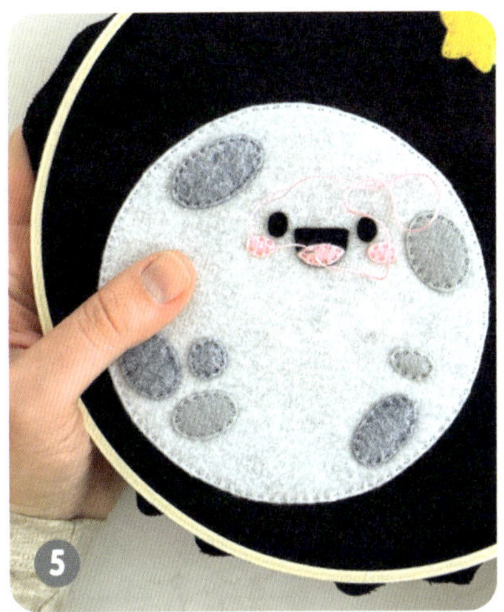
5

6

5. Add a face to the moon. Position the eyes, mouth, and cheeks. Use one strand of black floss to stitch a vertical line through the center of each eye and a running stitch around the outer edge of the mouth. Use one strand of pink floss to make a running stitch around the outer edge of each cheek. Keeping your needle threaded, position the tongue piece and use your pink floss to make a running stitch around the outer edge.

6. Add stars to the sky. Use a chalk pencil to mark scattered dots to represent stars in the sky. Choose about one-third of your dots and turn them into six-pointed stars (draw a vertical line with an "X" on top). Use three strands of light-gray floss to make French knots on each dot. For the six-pointed stars, use one strand of light-gray floss to stitch the center vertical line, followed by each arm of the "X."

working *with* kiddos

- **Allow your child to cut the moon and crater shapes.** Because these shapes are larger and don't require any fancy corner cutting, they make great practice pieces to hone kids' cutting skills. If your child is anything like mine and gets nervous about making mistakes, remind them that mistakes are part of the artistic process (and that you can help smooth things out if needed).
- **Give your child creative control with crater placement.** Part of the fun when stitching full moons is deciding where the craters should go! I've given you a starting point with my positioning, but maybe you want more craters (or fewer), or different colors or positioning. This step is a perfect one to open up to your child; give them final say on how many craters to have and where to put them.
- **Allow your child to draw the stars.** This is another step well suited to younger stitchers, because it really doesn't matter where the stars go or how many you have. Chalk pencils are easy to erase with a damp paper towel if needed, which makes this step relatively frustration-free.

If your child feels confident enough to try a project entirely on their own, this is a perfect one to start with!

buddies in bloom

One of my favorite things about spring is watching flowers bloom. I struggle to keep houseplants alive, so seeing nature do its own thing in such a spectacular way with no help from anyone is extra special for me. We have a small garden plot in our yard, and we always look forward to seeing the first crocuses and tulips pop up after tucking them into the cold earth the autumn before. Floral patterns are a common motif in traditional embroidery, but we'll be stitching flowers in a unique way with this project!

This pattern uses felt layering to give our flower bed depth and dimension. The color palette is bright and cheery, but if pink isn't your vibe, there's plenty of room to customize your garden with whatever flowers spark joy for you.

Templates on page 135.

supplies

- 8" (20 cm) embroidery hoop
- cotton fabric in light blue
- felt in colors shown at right
- 6-strand embroidery floss in colors: dark brown, copper, dark green, light green, dark pink, light pink, white, light yellow, black, dark yellow
- white felt for backing

tools

- embroidery needle
- straight pins
- scissors
- heat-erasable pen
- hot-glue gun

stitches used

- running stitch
- backstitch
- fly stitch
- French knot
- fill stitch

felt colors

- hazelnut
- umber
- conifer
- citron
- bellwether white
- custard
- canary
- bellwether black
- hibiscus
- begonia

buddies in bloom

1. Stitch the soil. Position the soil piece along the bottom edge of your hoop so that the top edge is level and straight, and pin it in place. Use one strand of dark-brown floss to make a running stitch along the outer edge of the piece. This piece sits flush against the edge of the hoop, so your stitches may not be as close to the edge of the felt when working along the bottom edge, and that's okay!

2. Stitch the flower-bed frame. Position the flower-bed frame along the bottom edge of your hoop so that the top edge is level and straight. Pin it in place. Use one strand of copper floss to make a running stitch around the outer edge of the piece.

3. Add detail to the flower-bed frame. Use a heat-erasable pen and a ruler to make two horizontal lines on the flower-bed frame. Make a few vertical lines in each row, staggering them to give the appearance of wood planks or bricks. Use one strand of copper floss to make long, straight backstitches for each horizontal row, ending each stitch at the base of a vertical line. Use that same copper floss to make one straight stitch for each vertical line.

4. Stitch the daisy bases and leaves. Position your daisy bases. You may wish to lay out all five flower bases to make sure things line up the way you want them to. Pin the daisies in the center of the flower part. Use one strand of dark-green floss to make a running stitch around the outer edge of the flower, down the center of the stem, and around the outer edge of each leaf. Position the leaf pieces and secure them with a single straight stitch, starting just below the outer point and finishing just above the inner point.

1

2

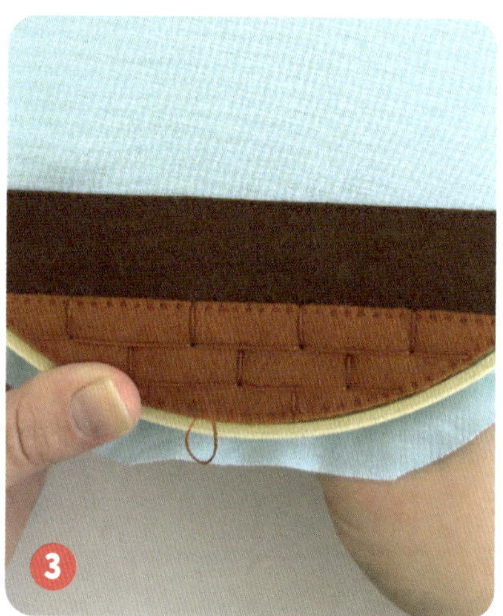

3

4

5. Stitch the tulip bases and leaves. Position the tulip bases and pin them in place through the flower portion. Repeat the process you used to stitch the daisy bases, using light-green floss this time. Position the leaf pieces and secure them with a single straight stitch, starting just below the outer point and finishing just above the inner point.

6. Stitch the flower petals. Now that the bases and leaves are in position, let's start stitching some flowers! Position each flower atop its base and pin in place. Use one strand of coordinating floss (dark pink, light pink, or white) to make a running stitch along the outer edge of each set of petals.

7. Stitch the daisy centers. Position the daisy center pieces on their flowers. These pieces may be too small to pin, so you may wish to stitch them one at a time. Use one strand of light-yellow floss to make a running stitch around the outer edge of the circle.

8. Add details to the flowers. Use a heat-erasable pen to draw eyes, cheeks, and a smile on each flower. Use two strands of black floss to fill in each eye and two strands of dark-yellow or either pink floss to fill each cheek. Refer to fill stitch on page 29 if needed. Backstitch the smiles. Finally, use two strands of dark-green and light-green floss to make a few fly-stitch weeds in the soil.

9. Stitch the cloud and bee bases. Position the cloud in the upper right of the hoop and pin in place. Use one strand of white floss to make a running stitch along the outer edge of the shape. For the bee bases, position them near the flowers and make a small horizontal tacking stitch in the center of the body with one strand of white floss. Make a vertical stitch down the center of each wing, ending your stitch below where the top edge of the body will be.

10. Stitch the bee bodies. Position the bee bodies on top of each base. These pieces will be too small to pin, so you may wish to stitch them one at a time. Use one strand of dark-yellow floss to make a running stitch along the outer edge of each body.

11. Stitch the bee stripes. Position the stripe vertically in the center of the bee's body. These pieces will be too small to pin, so you may wish to position just one at a time. Use one strand of black floss to make a running stitch along the outer edge of each stripe.

12. Add details to the bees. Use two strands of black floss to make a French-knot eye on each bee. Stitch the stinger by making a small "V" with two strands of black floss and filling in the shape with small horizontal stitches. Use a heat-erasable pen to draw a curving, dashed line from the stinger into a nearby flower. I like to add a small loop somewhere in mine! Use one strand of black floss to make a running stitch along this curve.

9

10

11

12

working *with* kiddos

- **Allow your child to decide on the color palette.** While it's fine to stick to the color palette I've provided, this is the perfect opportunity for your child to step in and take the reins. Maybe they prefer purple or orange tulips or want to make a whole rainbow garden! Allowing for flexibility in the color choices is a great way to make the project feel like it's really theirs (even if they aren't ready to do the bulk of the stitching just yet).

- **Allow your child to cut some of the more basic shapes.** The soil, flower-bed frame, flower petals, and cloud are all fairly large pieces without any sharp corners or intricate scissor work. Cutting these pieces would be a great way to include your child in the prep portion of this project (without risking the frustration that may come with trying to cut some of the narrower elements).

- **Put your child in charge of the garden insects.** The pattern as written includes bees, and it's easy to allow younger crafters to decide where the bees should go and how their paths should be drawn. Drawing those looping trails is a fun part of the process, and my own kids love to help here! If your child is feeling adventurous, maybe they want to try adding butterflies instead of (or in addition to) bees. I've included a simple butterfly shape in the templates for this pattern. Cut it out in the color of your choice and secure it to the hoop with a line of backstitches down the center. This leaves the wings free to fly!

If your child feels confident enough to try this project entirely on their own, let them know you're nearby for help if they need it!

fast-food friends

When it comes to food, there are some pairings that are just meant to be. These classic combinations are so iconic that it feels like they've been around since the beginning of time, although most are recent inventions. I'm talking about duos like peanut butter and jelly, macaroni and cheese, bacon and eggs, and (a favorite of mine) a burger and fries! National Burger Day is May 28, making this the perfect pair to stitch in the spring. I love bringing food items to life with little kawaii faces, which is exactly what we'll be doing with this project.

We'll be creating dimension in multiple ways here! We'll start by layering ingredients to create a pillowy, full-bodied burger, and then we'll add a thin layer of quilt batting to the fry box to give it more bulk (although this step is optional).

Templates on page 136.

supplies

- 8" (20 cm) embroidery hoop
- cotton fabric in bright blue
- felt in colors shown at right
- 6-strand embroidery floss in colors: dark brown, gold, bright red, green, light brown, black-brown, cream, pale yellow, white, bright yellow, magenta
- quilt batting (optional to add padding)
- white felt for backing

tools

- embroidery needle
- straight pins
- scissors
- heat-erasable pen
- hot-glue gun

stitches used

- running stitch
- backstitch
- detached chain stitch
- fill stitch
- couching stitch

felt colors

- hazelnut
- toast
- cherry red
- citron
- butterscotch
- bellwether white
- ochre
- cerise

fast-food friends

1. Stitch the burger base layer. Position both base layers in the center of your hoop and pin them in place. We'll be building the burger first and then moving over to the fries. Start by using one strand of dark-brown floss to make a running stitch around the outer edge of the burger base layer.

2. Stitch the cheese. Now we'll begin layering on the burger toppings. Position the cheese piece so that the top edge aligns with the burger base and pin it in place. Use one strand of gold floss to make a running stitch around the outer edge of the piece.

3. Stitch the tomato. Position the tomato piece so that the top edge aligns with the cheese and pin it in place. You should just be able to see the corners of the cheese sticking out from the bottom. Use one strand of bright-red floss to make a running stitch around the outer edge of the piece.

4. Stitch the lettuce. Position the lettuce piece so that the top edge aligns with the tomato and pin it in place. Use one strand of green floss to make a running stitch along the top arch of the lettuce piece. Leave the curvy part along the bottom edge unstitched to make your lettuce look extra lush and leafy!

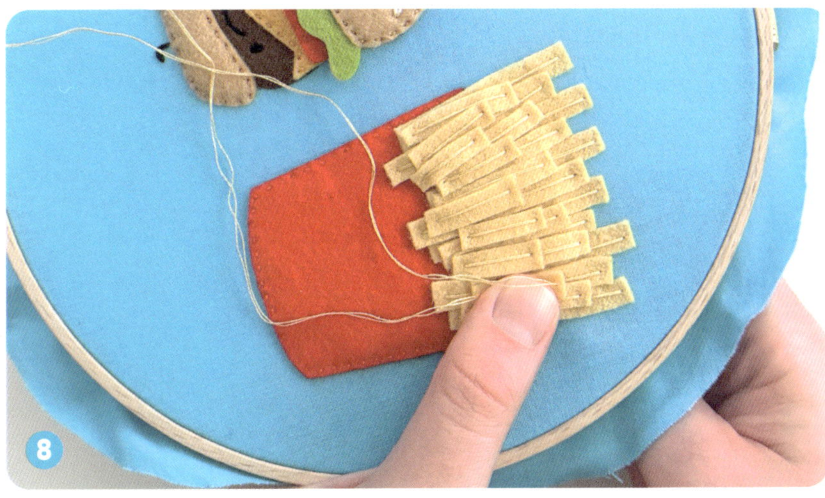

5. Stitch the burger buns. Position the top and bottom bun pieces and pin them in place. Use one strand of light-brown floss to make a running stitch along the outer edge of both buns. With all the ingredient layers we added, your top bun should look super full and fluffy.

6. Add details to the burger. Use a heat-erasable pen to draw a small face on the burger (I drew mine in the meat layer), to add legs and feet to the burger, and to plot out the sesame seeds on the top bun. Use two strands of black-brown floss to backstitch the mouth and fill in the eyes. Refer to fill stitch on page 29 if needed. Use two strands of black-brown floss to make a single straight stitch for each leg and to fill-stitch the feet (I like to make one straight stitch for the bottom of the foot and then a shorter stitch just above it). Use one strand of cream floss to make detached chain stitches for the sesame seeds.

7. Stitch the fry base layer. Now that the burger is complete, let's move on to stitching the fries! Your base layer is already pinned, so use one strand of bright-red floss to make a running stitch along the outer edge of the base layer.

8. Stitch the fries. Layer your fries in the fry box, starting with the longest fries at the back and working forward to the shortest fries. Because these pieces are so thin, we won't be pinning them, so you'll want to work slowly as you stitch. Use one strand of pale-yellow floss to make a single vertical stitch down the center of each fry.

9. Stitch the fry-box top. For this step, you may wish to add a layer of quilt batting for extra dimension (read more about this on page 125). If you're adding quilt batting, cut a piece in the same shape as the fry-box top. Layer these pieces together, position them on the hoop, and pin in place. Use one strand of bright-red floss to make a running stitch around the outer edge of the piece. (Note: If you're not using batting, simply pin your piece and stitch it without that extra layer.)

10. Stitch the stripe. Position the horizontal stripe on the fry box and pin it in place. It should land about a third of the way down from the top of the box. Use one strand of white floss to make a running stitch around the outer edge of the piece.

11. Add details to the fry box. Use a heat-erasable pen to draw a face near the bottom of the fry box, to add legs, and to mark out where you want your vertical stripes to go (I made small dots along the top and bottom edges so I knew where to place my couching stitches). Use two strands of black-brown floss to backstitch the mouth and fill in the eyes. Stitch the legs the same way you stitched the burger legs in step 6. Use one strand of bright-yellow floss to make vertical couching stitches along the length of the white stripe.

12. Stitch the heart. Position the heart between the burger and fries. It'll be too small to pin, so you'll want to work slowly and carefully as you stitch. Use one strand of magenta floss to make two detached chain stitches, one in each lobe of the heart. Begin and end your chains near the bottom point of the heart, so that your stitches create a smaller heart inside.

9

10

11

12

working *with* kiddos

- **Allow your child to cut the pieces.** The shapes in this piece are very kid-friendly! With the layering technique we're using for the burger, all the shapes are large with easy corners, and in the case of the fries, they're either large and easy or meant to be organic shapes anyway. The heart is a bit small and may be frustrating for younger children who aren't as confident with their scissors, but this is a great step to get your young stitchers involved in.

- **Put your child in charge of the layering.** Maybe your kiddo isn't interested in cutting pieces but is very invested in adding pieces to the hoop as you work. This layering technique is especially suited to young stitchers, because all the pieces align on at least one edge, making it easy to determine where they need to be. Allow your child to oversee the placement of the pieces, and maybe even help with the pinning! It's a great way to practice the layering and layout skills they'll need to complete projects on their own.

- **Allow your child to take over the details.** This pattern has such fun details! Between the cute little faces, the sesame seeds on the burger, and the pattern on the fry-box stripe, there are so many opportunities to let your kiddo take over and allow their creativity to shine. Give them free rein with the heat-erasable pen (and let them stitch those details themselves if they're feeling adventurous)!

This project lends itself so well to being completed by younger stitchers. If your child feels confident enough to try this project entirely on their own, let them know you're nearby for help if they need it!

beam me up

I remember the exact moment my style as an artist shifted. A few years ago, I made my husband a Doctor Strange portrait out of felt for Christmas. Before then, I had been making what I thought was beautiful work, but I didn't really consider myself an artist. With that Doctor Strange hoop, I used different shades of felt to create dimension and shading in my piece, and it finally clicked for me: I could do everything painters or illustrators do, but with felt.

I've grown a lot as an artist since then, and one of the effects that I'm the most proud of having created is the illusion of light. By using different shades in the same color family, we'll be creating that illusion here. It's a bit more challenging than what we've stitched so far, but I know you can do it.

Templates on pages 137–138.

supplies

- 8" (20 cm) embroidery hoop
- cotton fabric in eggplant purple
- felt in colors shown at right
- 6-strand embroidery floss in colors: light yellow, light gray, pale purple, dark gray, light purple, medium purple, black, dark purple, dusty purple, dark teal, medium teal, medium yellow, dark pink, dusty rose, light peach, light orange, light pink
- white felt for backing

tools

- embroidery needle
- straight pins
- scissors
- heat-erasable pen
- chalk pencil
- hot-glue gun

stitches used

- running stitch
- backstitch
- fly stitch
- French knot
- couching stitch

felt colors

- crema
- apricot
- plié
- custard
- canary
- viridian
- cerulean
- boysenberry
- orchid
- thistle
- lavender
- lunar
- ash
- black
- lilac
- Concord
- opal

1. Prepare the hill and bush pieces. To prepare the hills and bushes for stitching, we'll first need to cut them to the right shapes for our light effect. Lay out the moon, UFO base, and light beam to ensure that everything is positioned the way you want it, and pin these pieces in place. Next, we'll lay the lighter-purple hill pieces in their positions, over the top of the light beam. You'll be able to feel the light beam underneath; use a heat-erasable pen to draw the line of the light beam's edge on each of the hill pieces. Cut along this line. Use the scrap piece as a template to cut the right shape for your dark-purple hill piece. Repeat this process for the front hill and both bush pieces.

2. Stitch the light beam. With our base pieces pinned and our foliage ready to go, let's begin stitching the light beam. Use one strand of light-yellow floss to make a running stitch along the outer edge of the light-beam piece.

3. Stitch the UFO base. At this point, we're ready to begin assembling the UFO. Start by using one strand of light-gray floss to make a running stitch around the outer edge of the base piece.

4. Stitch the UFO metal bottom and the dome. Position the dome and rim pieces and pin them in place. The pieces should align along the central edges. Use one strand of pale-purple floss to make a running stitch around the outer edge of the dome and one strand of dark-gray floss to make a running stitch around the outer edge of the metal rim.

1

2

3

4

5. Add details to the UFO. Position the lights so that they're evenly spaced along the metal rim. Use one strand of coordinating floss (light purple and medium purple) to make a vertical stitch in the center of each light. Use one strand of dark-gray floss to make vertical couching stitches between each set of lights to bring more dimension to the rim. Position the eyes near the bottom of the dome and secure them in place with a single vertical stitch in the center with black floss. Use a heat-erasable pen to draw the mouth, centering it between the eyes, and backstitch it using two strands of black floss.

6. Stitch the hill bases. Position the hill pieces so that they align with the light beam and pin them in place. Use one strand of coordinating floss (dark purple and dusty purple) to stitch around the outer edge of each hill piece. To preserve the illusion of a beam of light shining on the hills, I recommend leaving the seams along the light beam unstitched.

7. Stitch the front hill. Position the pieces of the front hill and pin them in place. Use one strand of coordinating floss (dark purple and dusty purple) to make a running stitch along the top and bottom edges of each piece, leaving those seams where the light beam cuts through unstitched.

8. Stitch the bush bases. Position the bush pieces and pin them in place. Use one strand of coordinating floss (dark teal and medium teal) to stitch along the top and bottom edges, leaving the seams where the beam of light cuts through unstitched.

9. Add details to the hills and bushes. Position the small flowers on the hills. Secure each one with a yellow French knot in the center, keeping in mind that you should use the medium yellow for the flowers outside the light and the light yellow for those that fall within the light. Use two strands of dark-pink and dusty-rose floss to make fly-stitch plants on the hills. Use three strands of dark-pink and dusty-rose floss to make French-knot berries on the bushes. (You can mark these out with a heat-erasable pen first if that's easier.)

10. Stitch the moon base. Let's move on to the moon! Use one strand of light-peach floss to make a running stitch around the outer edge of the moon base.

11. Stitch the craters. To add the craters to your moon, position them on the moon base in whatever layout feels best to you. Use one strand of coordinating floss (light orange and light pink) to make a running stitch around the outer edge of each crater.

12. Stitch the stars. Position the yellow stars just below the UFO inside the beam of light. Secure them to the hoop by using one strand of medium-yellow floss to make straight stitches from the center of the star to the tip of each arm. Use a chalk pencil to position stars in the sky. If desired, turn a few of these into six-pointed stars. To stitch the six-pointed stars, use one strand of pale-purple floss to make the vertical stitch in the center, followed by an "X" over the top of it. To stitch the rest of the stars, use three strands of pale-purple floss to make a French knot for each star.

Tip:

My recommendation is to choose an odd-number amount, like 5, 7, or 9, when placing six-pointed stars. It's more visually pleasing to our eye than an even number!

working *with* kiddos

- **Allow your child to decide on the color palette or the foliage.** This is the perfect step to allow your child to take the reins. I've stitched a similar UFO in blues and greens with trees below it, and I honestly can't decide which one I like better! Especially if this is a project that will be going in a child's room, it would be fun to coordinate the color palette with themes you already have in your space, and tree shapes are very easy to freehand!

- **Allow your child to cut some of the more basic shapes.** While the stars, craters, and UFO eyes are quite small, the rest of the pieces in this pattern would be fairly easy for little hands to cut out on their own. I'm a big believer in allowing children to help in every stage of the project, especially for pieces that will end up in their spaces, and this is a great way to include them in the prep stage.

- **Put your child in charge of the layout decisions.** There are many elements in this piece that are laid out according to your own personal preference (such as the flowers, craters, and stars in the sky). Why not allow your child to be creative director for these steps? Allow them to decide where everything should go and how to space it all. This will give them a strong sense of involvement, even if you're the one doing the bulk of the stitching.

This is considered an intermediate pattern because of the light beam and the prep work that goes into creating that illusion, but if your child feels confident enough to try this project entirely on their own, let them know you're nearby for help if they need it!

under the sea

One of my favorite childhood memories is the day my mom called us all out from school so that we could drive along the Washington coast, watching for the gray whale migration that was supposed to be visible from the shore. We didn't see any whales that day, but it still felt so magical and remains a core memory for me. Whales are stunning creatures, majestic ocean ballerinas that I've loved since I was very small. From the social structures of orcas to the bubble net feeding of humpback whales to the sheer unfathomable size of blue whales, there are so many wonderful things to learn about this group of animals.

This friendly design is a perfect choice for anyone looking for a project they can complete in an afternoon, or for very young stitchers looking for a first project to tackle on their own.

Templates on page 139.

supplies

- 8" (20 cm) embroidery hoop
- cotton fabric in dark blue
- felt in colors shown at right
- 6-strand embroidery floss in colors: light blue, dark blue, black, peach, light orange, medium orange, greenish-blue
- white felt for backing

tools

- embroidery needle
- straight pins
- scissors
- heat-erasable pen
- chalk pencil
- hot-glue gun

stitches used

- running stitch
- whipped backstitch
- fly stitch
- French knot

felt colors

- salmon
- dreamsicle
- crema
- Capri
- sea mist
- bellwether black

1. Stitch the whale base. Position the whale base in the hoop, centering it as much as possible (my whale has a little bit more space above it than below). Pin the base piece in place. Use one strand of light-blue floss to make a running stitch around the outer edge of the piece.

2. Stitch the whale top layer. Position the whale's top layer and pin it in place. The tail shape and the curve along the top of the whale are the same as the base, so you can use those as your guides for placement. Use one strand of dark-blue floss to make a running stitch around the outer edge of the piece.

3. Add the fin, eye, cheek, and blowhole. Position the fin and pin in place. Use one strand of dark-blue floss to make a running stitch around the outer edge of the piece. Position the eye and cheek near the fin and the blowhole near the top curve of the whale's body, slightly forward from the eye. Use one strand of coordinating floss (black, peach, and dark blue) to make a single stitch in the center of each of these ovals (vertical for the eye, horizontal for the cheek and blowhole).

4. Stitch the smaller ocean friends. Position the fish and octopuses around the whale in whatever positions feel best to you. They'll be a little too small to pin, so it's up to you whether you work one piece at a time or add them all at once and just work slowly and carefully. Use one strand of coordinating floss (peach, light orange, and medium orange) to make a running stitch around the outer edge of each sea creature.

1

2

3

4

5. Add eyes and smiles to each of the sea creatures. Use a heat-erasable pen to draw an eye on each fish and eyes and a small smile on each octopus. Use two strands of black floss to make French knots for each eye. (If you want a slightly larger eye, you can wrap your floss three times instead of two times.) Use those same two strands of black floss to make a small fly-stitch mouth for each octopus.

6. Stitch the bubbles. Use a chalk pencil to trace bubbles all over your hoop. Be sure to use a variety of different sizes to add visual interest to your piece! I drew 21 bubbles, because there are three shades of blue floss to use (light blue, dark, blue, and greenish-blue) and 21 is a multiple of three, but the exact number is up to you. Use two strands of floss to stitch each bubble with a whipped backstitch. This process takes a while, but the result is so satisfying!

working *with* kiddos

- **Put your child in charge of cutting the pieces.** This piece has larger, easier-to-cut pieces than some of the other patterns in this book. This would be the perfect opportunity to allow your child to practice this skill if they're interested! The smaller pieces (the eye, cheek, and blowhole) may be a bit tricky for little makers, but the rest should be fairly easy.

- **Let your child be in charge of the sea creatures.** If there are any placement decisions that aren't specific to the tutorial (things like stars, snowflakes, sparkles, bubbles, clouds, etc.), I love handing those decisions over to my kids. It's a great way to make them feel included, even if they don't want to stitch anything themselves. Let your child decide where to place the fish and octopuses. If they want to add more sea creatures, or design their own, those are great options as well!

- **Let your child add the bubbles.** How many bubbles should you have, and where should they all go? This is the perfect step for young children to weigh in on! They could even trace the bubbles themselves, as circles are a very simple shape (if desired, the bubbles could also be freehanded for more variety).

This project is a fantastic one to start with for new stitchers. If your child feels confident enough to try this project entirely on their own, let them know you're nearby for help if they need it!

serene shore

I love turning inanimate objects, especially buildings and structures, into characters for my designs. In my experience, seeing different foods, plants, or animals with cute little kawaii faces is a common experience, but buildings are a bit rarer. One of my favorite hoop designs in recent years was a windmill surrounded by tulips, and I knew I wanted to bring at least one unusual character to this book.

Enter the lighthouse! My best friend growing up lived near the shores of Lake Michigan, and there were lighthouses aplenty to visit on our summer vacations. Lighthouses are an iconic symbol of guidance and safety, and this design is so soothing that I can practically hear the gulls and smell the salty air.

Templates on page 140.

supplies

- 8" (20 cm) embroidery hoop
- cotton fabric in sky blue
- felt in colors shown at right
- 6-strand embroidery floss in colors: dark blue, light green, white, red, dark green, copper, light brown, black-brown, beige, light yellow, light pink, light blue
- white felt for backing

tools

- embroidery needle
- straight pins
- scissors
- heat-erasable pen
- hot-glue gun

stitches used

- running stitch
- backstitch
- fly stitch
- French knot
- couching stitch

felt colors

- chicory
- umber
- toast
- oyster
- plié
- cherry red
- sesame
- wasabi
- conifer
- cerulean
- bellwether white

1. Stitch the water layer. Position the water layer so that the bottom curved edge aligns with the bottom edge of the hoop and the horizontal straight edge is level. Pin the piece in place. Use one strand of dark-blue floss to make a running stitch around the outer edge of the piece.

2. Add the clifftop. Position the clifftop along the left side of the ocean. The bottom curved edge should completely cover the blue beneath, and the top horizontal edge should be level. Pin the piece in place. Use one strand of light-green floss to make a running stitch around the outer edge of the piece.

3. Stitch the lighthouse base. Let's start assembling our lighthouse! Position the lighthouse-base piece so that it overlaps the lighthouse shape attached to the clifftop piece. Pin in place. Use one strand of white floss to make a running stitch around the outer edge of the piece.

4. Add the bands of color to the lighthouse. Lay out the colored bands so that the stripes alternate between red and white. If you need to do any trimming so that the edges align, now is the time to do it. Pin the bands in place. Use one strand of coordinating floss (white and red) to make a running stitch around the outer edge of each band.

1

2

3

4

5

6

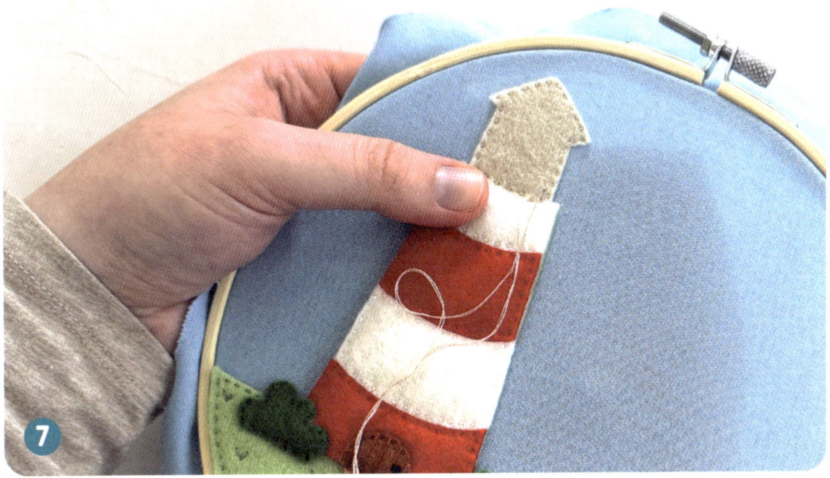

7

5. Stitch the bushes, door, and path. Position the bushes, door, and path pieces. The bushes will align with the bumpy shapes of the clifftop piece, and the door will be centered in the bottom band of the lighthouse, with the bottom edge aligned with the bottom edge of the lighthouse. Position the path so that the narrow end is just below the bottom edge of the door. Pin the path in place (the other pieces are too small to pin). Use one strand of coordinating floss (dark green, copper, and light brown) to make a running stitch around the outer edge of each piece.

6. Add detail to the door and grass. To add detail to the door, use a heat-erasable pen to mark four or five evenly spaced dots along the top edge of the door. Use one strand of copper floss to make vertical couching stitches at each of these dots. Use two strands of black-brown floss to make a French-knot doorknob. Use a heat-erasable pen to mark out several small "V" shapes in the grass, and use two strands of light-green floss to make fly-stitch weeds.

7. Stitch the upper section of the lighthouse. Now that the main part of the structure is complete, it's time to build the upper section of the lighthouse. Position the top structure piece so that the curved bottom edge aligns with the curved top edge of the lighthouse bands. Pin in place. Use one strand of beige floss to make a running stitch around the outer edge of the piece.

8. Add the roof and light. Position the roof piece and hold it in place with your nondominant thumb. Use one strand of copper floss to make a running stitch around the outer edge of the piece. Once the roof is finished, position the light so that it's centered in the remaining space. Hold it in place with your nondominant thumb and use one strand of light-yellow floss to make a running stitch around the outer edge of the piece.

9. Stitch the railing and roof detail. Use a heat-erasable pen to draw two horizontal curved lines on the rooftop. Make a single vertical line centered in the middle section and two vertical lines breaking the bottom section into thirds. This creates the appearance of shingles on the roof piece. Use one strand of copper floss to stitch each vertical line with a single stitch, and backstitch the curved horizontal lines. Use your heat-erasable pen to draw a curved line a few millimeters above the bottom edge of the upper section. Draw several vertical lines along the length of this line. Use one strand of black-brown floss to stitch each vertical line and to backstitch the curved line. This will create your railing!

Tip:

Don't forget to make two small stitches between each end of the railing and the upper section of the lighthouse, to make it look like the railing extends all the way around.

10. Stitch the lighthouse face. Position the eyes and cheeks in the lower white band (third down from the top). Use a heat-erasable pen to draw a curved smile between the eyes. Use one strand of coordinating floss (black-brown and light pink) to secure each eye and cheek with a single stitch in the center (vertical for the eyes, horizontal for the cheeks). Use two strands of black-brown floss to backstitch the mouth.

11. Add detail to the ocean. Use a heat-erasable pen to draw curved shapes to represent waves in the ocean. Use two strands of dark-blue floss to backstitch each of these curves. Once complete, use two strands of light-blue floss to make a second row of backstitches above the dark blue, to give the waves a bit of dimension and help them stand out.

12. Stitch the clouds and birds. Position the clouds in the sky. I added one of the smaller clouds to the space on the left of the lighthouse and used a heat-erasable pen to mark where I needed to trim it down. Pin each cloud in place and use one strand of white floss to make a running stitch around the edge of each cloud. Use a heat-erasable pen to draw curved "V" shapes in the sky to represent flying birds. Use two strands of black-brown floss to backstitch each bird.

working *with* kiddos

- **Allow your child to practice their running stitch.** This piece has a lot of opportunity to practice running stitch on large and simple shapes. The ocean, clifftop, lighthouse base, and lighthouse bands are all large with no sharp corners to work around. The clouds would also be great pieces to practice on if your child would rather join in toward the end of the project!
- **Let your child decide on the weed and wave placements.** Hand over the pen and let your child decide where this accent stitching should happen. How many waves will be in the ocean? Will they be large or small? How much embellishment should the grass have? These are easy shapes to draw and are a great way to include your child in the process.
- **Put your child in charge of the sky.** This is another fun way to include your child in the project. How many clouds should be in the sky? How many birds? Where should everything go? This is a great opportunity to teach your kiddo about asymmetry, and the fact that things look more organic and visually pleasing in odd numbers.

If your child feels confident enough to try this project entirely on their own, let them know you're nearby for help if they need it!

merry mermaid

Of all the mythical creatures, a mermaid was the one I most wanted to be as a kid. My dad was in the Navy, so I spent much of my childhood on or around water and took every opportunity to pretend I could breathe underwater and talk to fish. Mermaids have been a prominent part of folklore in many cultures for centuries, and society's love for them doesn't appear to be dwindling at all, as they still feature heavily in books and movies. That might be how I've passed the mermaid fascination down to my daughter (who was ecstatic that I'm including a mermaid in my book).

Some of my very favorite Benzie shades are featured in this pattern (hibiscus, coral, and teal are such a treat to work with), and I'm excited to share my process for creating long, beautiful hair with felt.

Templates on page 141.

supplies

- 8" (20 cm) embroidery hoop
- cotton fabric in light purple
- felt in colors shown at right
- 6-strand embroidery floss in colors: dark pink, tan, light purple, dark teal, medium teal, coral, black-brown, light pink, dark purple, yellow, medium blue, light blue
- white felt for backing

tools

- embroidery needle
- straight pins
- scissors
- heat-erasable pen
- hot-glue gun

stitches used

- running stitch
- backstitch
- fly stitch
- French knot
- fill stitch

felt colors

- hibiscus
- coral
- tellina
- chicory
- seaside
- Mikado
- julep
- teal
- Capri
- Nordic
- allium

merry mermaid

1. Stitch the base layer. Position the mermaid base layer, centering it as much as possible. Because of the unusual shape, it may feel slightly off-center on the horizontal axis, but whatever position feels best to you is perfect! Pin the piece in place. Use one strand of dark-pink floss to make a running stitch around the outer edge of the piece.

2. Add the skin layer. Position the skin layer over the base layer so that the tail section aligns with the base. Pin the piece in place. Use one strand of tan floss to make a running stitch around the outer edge of the piece.

3. Stitch the head and bralette. Position the head and pin in place. Use one strand of tan floss to make a running stitch around the outer edge of the piece. Position the bralette so that the top corners align with the armpits. Hold in place with your nondominant thumb and use one strand of light-purple floss to make a running stitch around the outer edge of the piece.

4. Stitch the tail and fin. Position the tail and tail fin so that they align with the layers beneath and pin them in place. The tip of the tail should slide into the cutout of the fin piece. Use one strand of coordinating floss (dark teal and medium teal) to make a running stitch around the outer edge of each piece.

5. Stitch the front hair sections. Position the front sections of hair so that the straight edges meet in the center and the outer curved edges align with the base piece. Use one strand of coral floss to make a running stitch around the outer edges of the pieces, leaving the inside edges unstitched. This gives the hair more movement!

6. Add the hair contrast pieces. Position the contrast pieces in their respective sections (piece 1 goes on the right, piece 2 goes on the left, and piece 3 goes under the left arm). Hold the piece in place with your nondominant thumb and use contrasting floss (coral and dark pink) to backstitch a line in the center of the piece, following the curve of the shape. Repeat for the other two pieces.

7. Add detail to the hair and tail. Use a heat-erasable pen to draw a few curved lines on the base layer of hair. Use two strands of coral floss to backstitch each of the lines. Use your heat-erasable pen to mark out "V" shapes down the length of the tail, and use two strands of dark-teal floss to make fly-stitch scales.

8. Stitch the starfish. Position the starfish in the right section of hair, near the top of the head. Use two strands of dark-pink floss to make small French knots over the surface of the starfish to secure it to the mermaid.

9. Stitch the mermaid's face. Position the mouth near the bottom edge of the head and use one strand of black-brown floss to make a single horizontal stitch near the top of the mouth. Use a heat-erasable pen to draw two vertical eyes, a horizontal nose, and two horizontal cheeks. Use fill stitches to stitch each of these facial features (in black-brown, tan, and light pink). Position the tongue so that it aligns with the bottom curve of the mouth and secure it using one strand of dark-pink floss to make a single horizontal stitch in the center.

9

10. Add detail to the bralette and stitch the fish. Use a heat-erasable pen to draw three curved lines on each side of the bralette. Use one strand of dark-purple floss to backstitch each of these curved lines. Position the fish to the left and right of the mermaid and use one strand of yellow floss to make a running stitch around the outer edge of each fish.

10

11. Add eyes to the fish. Use a heat-erasable pen to mark a dot for each fish's eye. Use two to three strands of black-brown floss to make a French-knot eye for each fish. The number of strands will determine the size of the eye, so choose what feels best for the look you're going for (I used three).

11

12. Stitch the bubbles. To finish off this design, we just need to add a few bubbles to the scene. Position the bubbles around the mermaid. Use one strand of coordinating floss (medium blue and light blue) to make a running stitch around the outer edge of each bubble.

12

working *with* kiddos

- **Put your child in charge of the mermaid's hair.** Long, flowing hair is so much fun to bring to life with felt! I love cutting the little locks of hair that add dimension and layering them to make things look as realistic as possible. Bring your child in as a mermaid stylist and let them decide where to place all those detail pieces and where the backstitched strands should go.
- **Let your child decorate the tail and bralette.** Hand over the heat-erasable pen and allow your child some creative freedom with the mermaid's accent details! Maybe they have a different idea for the bralette or want to add some lines to the tail fin. Maybe they'd rather do French-knot scales instead of fly-stitch scales. Let their creativity shine for this part of the process and see what they come up with.
- **Put your child in charge of the bubbles.** There's no right or wrong way to lay out the bubbles in this design. I used a total of nine in various sizes, but there's plenty of space for more (or fewer, if you so choose). Put your child in charge of deciding on the number and placement of the bubbles. If they're feeling confident, they could even stitch the bubbles on their own.

This design involves a few small pieces and requires drawing a face, but if your child feels confident enough to try this project entirely on their own, let them know you're nearby for help if they need it!

let's taco 'bout it

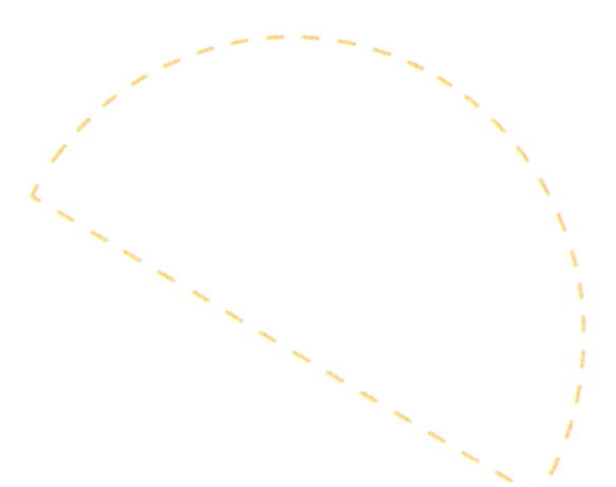

Tacos are my absolute favorite food in the whole world. The word "taco" translates to "light lunch," and tacos have been around in some form for centuries. The fillings vary depending on the region, but the format is the same: a simple tortilla filled with delicious toppings. I've sampled a great many, in various locations and from different restaurants, and I have never had a taco I didn't enjoy. Naturally, tacos needed to make their appearance in this book, and, since the first-ever food truck was most likely a taco truck, a cute little taco truck of my own was the perfect way to make that happen!

This design has a lot of pieces, but don't let that intimidate you. We'll be building our taco truck one layer at a time, in perfectly manageable bite-sized steps.

Templates on pages 142–143.

supplies

- 8" (20 cm) embroidery hoop
- cotton fabric in teal
- felt in colors shown at right
- 6-strand embroidery floss in colors: dark orange, white, dark brown, light orange, medium green, dark yellow, cream, black, red, dark pink, medium pink, medium yellow, gray, beige, black-brown
- white felt for backing

tools

- embroidery needle
- straight pins
- scissors
- heat-erasable pen
- hot-glue gun

stitches used

- running stitch
- backstitch
- French knot

felt colors

- chicory
- hazelnut
- shortbread
- tellina
- coral
- carmine
- clementine
- dreamsicle
- sesame
- canary
- golden
- citron
- lunar
- bellwether black
- bellwether white

1. Stitch the truck base, posts, and taco meat. Position the truck base, posts, and taco meat layer in the hoop. We'll be treating this entire base layer as a whole, so take a moment to make sure everything is centered. Use one strand of coordinating floss (dark orange, white, and dark brown) to make a running stitch around the outer edge of the taco meat and the truck, and make a single horizontal stitch at the top and bottom of each post. (Note: Don't forget to make a running stitch around the truck's window as well!)

2. Stitch the truck's lower half and the taco lettuce. Position the lighter lower half of the truck so that the bottom edge aligns with the bottom edge of the truck base. Pin in place. Position the taco-lettuce layer so that the bottom edge aligns with the bottom edge of the meat layer. Pin in place. Use one strand of coordinating floss (light orange and medium green) to make a running stitch around the outer edge of each piece.

3. Stitch the sauce drip, window base, and taco shell. Position the window-base layer and taco-shell pieces. The bottom edge of the window will slide right into the top edge of the truck's lower half, and the bottom edge of the taco shell will align with the bottom edge of the lettuce layer. Pin both pieces in place. Use one strand of coordinating floss (dark yellow and cream) to make a running stitch around the outer edge of each piece. The sauce drip pieces align with the top edge of the truck's lower half. These pieces will be too narrow to pin, so you'll need to work slowly and carefully to make sure they stay properly aligned. Use one strand of red floss to make a running stitch around the outer edge of each piece.

1

2

3

4

4. Add the taco face and lights. Time to add some personality to our taco mascot! Position the eyes, cheeks, and mouth so that the face is centered on the taco shell. Use one strand of coordinating floss (black and dark pink) to make a single vertical stitch in the center of each eye and a single horizontal stitch in the center of each cheek. Use one strand of black floss to make a running stitch around the mouth piece. Position the taillight and hold it in place with your nondominant thumb. Use one strand of medium pink to make a running stitch around the outer edge. Repeat this process for the headlight, using cream floss.

5. Stitch the wheel base, jaguar base, and menu. Now that the taco mascot and the bulk of the truck are done, let's move on to a few fine details. Position the wheel-base pieces, menu board, and jaguar-base piece. Pin each of these pieces in place. Use one strand of coordinating floss (black, medium yellow, and white) to make a running stitch around the outer edge of each piece.

6. Add the hubcaps and wheel covers. To finish off the wheels, position the wheel covers. These pieces will be too narrow to pin in place, so you'll need to work slowly and carefully while checking their positions often. Use one strand of dark-yellow floss to make a running stitch around the outer edge of each wheel well. Position the hubcap pieces and hold them in place with your nondominant thumb. Use one strand of gray floss to make a running stitch around the outer edge of each hubcap.

7. Stitch the jaguar body and add to the menu. Let's move on to the window now! Position the jaguar body and pin it in place. Use one strand of medium-yellow floss to make a running stitch around the outer edge of the piece. Position the taco-base and burrito-base layers on the menu. Use one strand of coordinating floss (medium green and beige) to make a running stitch around the lower half of the burrito and make a single horizontal stitch on the taco base layer.

8. Add detail to the menu board. Position the taco top layer and use one strand of dark-yellow floss to make a running stitch around the outer edge of the piece. Use two strands of floss to make French-knot fillings on the top portion of the burrito base. I used dark brown, medium green, and red for meat, lettuce, and tomatoes, but feel free to choose your favorite toppings! Use two strands of black-brown floss to make two horizontal lines to the side of each menu option.

9. Stitch the jaguar's head and apron. All that's left to do now is finish off our little jaguar friend! Position the head piece and pin it in place. Use one strand of medium-yellow floss to make a running stitch around the outer edge of the piece. Position the apron piece, and either pin or hold in place with your nondominant thumb. Use one strand of medium-green floss to make a running stitch around the outer edge.

9

Tip:

The more layers of felt you've added to a piece, the tougher it gets to pin pieces in place. At this stage, our jaguar technically consists of four layers. Don't be alarmed if you find it difficult to get pins in! These pieces are small enough to hold in place with your nondominant thumb if that's easiest.

10. Add detail to the apron and stitch the hat base. Position the tag piece near the top of the apron, centering it on the horizontal axis. Use two strands of black-brown floss to make a horizontal line in the center of the tag. Use those same two strands of black-brown floss to make vertical stitches from the top corners of the apron to the shoulders. Position the hat base and hold it in place with your nondominant thumb while you make a running stitch with one strand of white floss.

10

Tip:

If you want your apron strings to stand out more, make them the same color as the apron!

11. Stitch the jaguar's face and hat brim. Position the hat brim and use one strand of white floss to make a running stitch along the length of the brim, centering your stitches on the piece. Use that same single strand of white floss to make four stitches on the top of the hat, starting at the top point and angling down toward the brim. This gives the hat a bit more dimension! Position the mouth piece and use one strand of black-brown floss to make a single horizontal stitch in the center of the piece. Use a heat-erasable pen

11

12

to draw an inverted triangle nose and two eyes. Use two strands of black-brown floss to stitch the eyes with a fill stitch. Use two strands of medium-pink floss to make three horizontal stitches, making the stitch length shorter from top to bottom to fill in the triangle shape.

12. **Add detail to the jaguar.** Use two strands of medium-pink floss to make a few vertical stitches in each ear, angling the stitches to create a small triangle shape. Use a heat-erasable pen to draw whiskers and spots on the jaguar. Use two strands of black-brown floss to backstitch the whiskers. Continue using those two strands of black-brown floss to make a French knot for each spot.

working *with* kiddos

- **Allow your child to practice their running stitch.** The base layer of the truck, as well as the three layers of the taco mascot, are all great shapes to practice running stitch for newer (or younger) stitchers. These are the largest pieces in the design, and none of them have tight corners or sharp angles to trip beginners up. This would be the perfect opportunity to build some stitching confidence!

- **Put your child in charge of the menu.** My taco truck sells a basic taco and a burrito, but maybe your little helper has other foods in mind! Give them a chance to put their creativity to the test with designing items for the menu. Alternatively, if they'd rather not design anything new, you could put them in charge of positioning and deciding on the colors for the burrito fillings. These choices still give them the opportunity to make some creative decisions without added pressure.

- **Let your child add the jaguar details.** Does your kiddo have a different idea for the jaguar's uniform? Do they want to be in charge of placing the marks for the jaguar's spots? Hand over the heat-erasable pen and let them make some of these detail decisions! I'm all about empowering your child in small steps as they show interest. All these little moments of creative confidence will add up over time.

This pattern is considered intermediate because it involves a lot of pieces, many of them quite small. Some younger stitchers may find this overwhelming or intimidating, and that's okay. That said, if your child feels confident enough to try this project entirely on their own, let them know you're nearby for help if they need it!

magical mushroom terrarium

There are an estimated 14,000 varieties of mushroom in the world. Neither a plant nor an animal, mushrooms play an important role in the life cycles of various ecosystems. Mushrooms are not only fascinating organisms but also a staple in the cozy cottagecore aesthetic (which is 100 percent my vibe). They feature heavily in autumnal décor but, with the right color palette, can bring a touch of whimsy, magic, and mystery all year long.

There is truly not a more iconic mushroom than the red-spotted toadstool. As someone who enjoys incorporating mushrooms into our seasonal décor, there is no way I would have been able to write a book without including at least one mushroom, and I'm so excited to share this one with you.

Templates on pages 144–145.

supplies

- 8" (20 cm) embroidery hoop
- cotton fabric in light brown
- felt in colors shown at right
- 6-strand embroidery floss in colors: beige, cream, red, green, dark brown, black-brown, pink, gray, yellow
- white felt for backing

tools

- embroidery needle
- straight pins
- scissors
- heat-erasable pen
- hot-glue gun

stitches used

- running stitch
- backstitch
- whipped backstitch
- chain stitch
- French knot

felt colors

- chicory
- hazelnut
- oyster
- garnet
- bellwether ecru
- zucchini

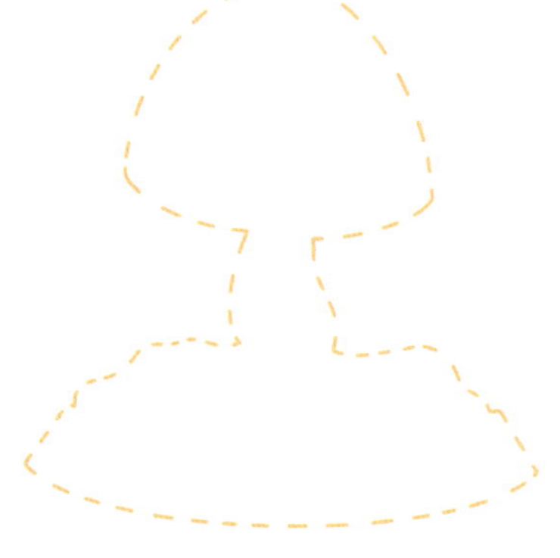

MUSHROOM

magical mushroom terrarium

1. Trace the terrarium outline and stitch the base layer. Center the terrarium outline in the hoop and trace with a heat-erasable pen. This will provide a guide for positioning felt pieces and also for chain-stitching later. Position the mushroom-base layer so that the bottom edge is just inside the bottom edge of the terrarium guideline and pin it in place. Use one strand of beige floss to make a running stitch around the outer edge of the piece.

2. Stitch the stem layer. Position the stem layer and pin it in place. This layer adds depth and dimension to the mushroom by highlighting the stem and pushing the underside of the mushroom cap to the background. Use one strand of cream floss to make a running stitch around the outer edge of the piece.

3. Stitch the mushroom cap, moss, and terrarium base. Position the mushroom-cap, moss, and terrarium-base pieces and pin each one in place. Because none of these overlap, we can stitch them all in the same phase! Use one strand of coordinating floss (red, green, and dark brown) to make a running stitch around the outer edge of each piece.

4. Add detail to the mushroom and stitch the small mushrooms. Use a heat-erasable pen to draw curved lines on the underside of the mushroom cap and use one strand of beige floss to backstitch each line. Position the mushroom spots and use one strand of cream floss to make a running stitch around the outer edge of each spot. To stitch the mushroom face, position the mouth toward the bottom of the stem, and use one strand of black-brown floss to secure it with a single stitch in the center. Use a heat-erasable pen to draw small eyes and cheeks. Use two strands of black-brown floss and a fill stitch for the eyes, and two strands of pink floss and a fill stitch for the cheeks. Position the small mushroom caps to the left and right of the larger mushroom stem. Use one strand of beige floss to make a running stitch around each piece. Use a heat-erasable pen to draw a small, curved stem under each mushroom cap, and use one strand of beige floss to stitch each stem with a whipped backstitch.

Tip:

You may find it easiest to work one spot at a time, since these pieces are too small to pin. You can either lay them all out and work slowly and carefully or lay them all out to get a sense of where to put them, then remove any that you're not actively stitching and add them one at a time.

5. Add detail to the terrarium base. Center the label piece on the terrarium base. This piece may be difficult to pin, so hold it in place with your nondominant thumb as you make a running stitch with one strand of beige floss. Use a heat-erasable pen to write the word "mushroom" on the label. Use two strands of black-brown floss to backstitch the lettering. Use a heat-erasable pen to mark out three dots to the left and right of the label. Use three strands of beige floss to make a French knot on each dot.

6. Chain-stitch the terrarium glass and add sparkles. Use two strands of gray floss to chain-stitch the terrarium glass. Begin your stitches at the top left corner of the terrarium base and finish at the top right corner of the terrarium base, leaving the lines around the base itself unstitched. Use a heat-erasable pen to mark sparkles inside the terrarium glass. You can use a mix of six-pointed stars and dots or do all of one or the other. Stitch any six-pointed stars with one strand of yellow or cream floss, and any French knots with three strands of yellow or cream floss.

Tip:

If you're not confident in your freehand lettering abilities, practice on paper first! I marked the halfway point of the label with my heat-erasable pen and then added four letters to either side. Alternatively, you could do some simple horizontal lines or just leave the label blank.

working *with* kiddos

- **Put your child in charge of cutting the pieces.** This piece has larger, easier-to-cut pieces than some of the other patterns in this book. This would be the perfect opportunity to allow your child to practice this skill if they're interested! The only piece that may be a bit tricky is the mouth, which is very small, but they may find that easier with smaller hands.
- **Allow your child to design the terrarium base.** I've shown you my version of the terrarium base in this tutorial, but maybe your little helper has other ideas. Stripes, six-pointed stars, a different word in the label—there are so many options to choose from when it comes to designing the base. This is the perfect opportunity to let their creativity shine!
- **Let your child add the sparkle.** Hand over the heat-erasable pen and let them decide how much magic lives inside this terrarium (and where all those sparkles should go)! Especially if cutting or stitching feels intimidating, this is a great step for them to dip their toe in the artistic pool and maybe build some momentum for future projects.

This project is a great one to start with for new stitchers. If your child feels confident enough to try this project entirely on their own, let them know you're nearby for help if they need it!

trick or treat

In the past, October was always a stressful month for me. The fact is, I am a giant scaredy cat, and horror and I do not mix. An entire month where society at large seems intent on terrifying me at every turn has never been my favorite thing, but, in recent years, my perspective has begun to change. Social media gives us the opportunity to curate our experience, and I've found many artists leaning more into the cute (rather than scary) side of spooky. I've found a lot of inspiration in that and now have more enjoyable Octobers.

The vibrant pumpkin bucket full of treats and the whimsical bats in the sky make this scene more cute than scary—just how I like it—and I hope you enjoy letting a little Halloween spirit creep in with this piece.

Templates on pages 146–147.

supplies

- 8" (20 cm) embroidery hoop
- cotton fabric in dark brown
- felt in colors shown at right
- 6-strand embroidery floss in colors: medium green, medium gray, dark gray, blue-gray, dark green, light yellow, black, cream, black-brown, light pink, dark orange, dark brown, magenta, red, dark yellow, bright green
- quilt batting (optional to add padding)
- white felt for backing

tools

- embroidery needle
- straight pins
- scissors
- heat-erasable pen
- hot-glue gun

stitches used

- running stitch
- backstitch
- fly stitch
- French knot
- couching stitch

felt colors

- chicory
- plié
- Chantenay
- sesame
- bellwether ecru
- meadow
- nori
- morel
- terrazzo
- slate
- bellwether black

1. Stitch the grass layer. Position the grass layer so that the bottom curve aligns with the bottom edge of your hoop and the top edge is level horizontally. Pin the piece in place. Use one strand of medium-green floss to make a running stitch around the outer edge of the shape.

2. Add the sidewalk. Position the sidewalk piece the same way you did the grass (the bottom curve should align with the bottom edge of your hoop and the top edge should be level horizontally). Pin the sidewalk in place and use one strand of medium-gray floss to make a running stitch around the outer edge of the piece. Before tying off, make three vertical stitches to segment the sidewalk.

3. Stitch the lamp base, reaper base, and bush. Position the lamp-base, reaper-base, and bush pieces. You may wish to pad the bush with a layer of quilt batting, but it's not necessary (see page 125 for more details). Pin each piece in place and stitch each one with a single strand of coordinating floss (dark gray, blue-gray, and dark green) and a running stitch around the outer edge.

4. Stitch the lamppost bottom, box, and bulb. Let's add some detail to the lamppost. These pieces are all fairly small or thin, so we won't be using pins at all. Working one piece at a time, use one strand of coordinating floss (dark gray, medium gray, and light yellow) to make a running stitch around the edge of the lamppost bottom, box, and bulb pieces.

1

2

3

4

5

6

5. Add the top to the lamppost. To finish off the lamppost, all that's left to add is the roof piece. This piece is also too small to be pinned but is easy to keep in place with the thumb on your nondominant hand. Use one strand of dark-gray floss to make a running stitch around the outer edge of the piece.

6. Stitch the reaper's body and head. Position the reaper body piece and head piece. Pin both in place. Use one strand of coordinating floss (black and cream) to make a running stitch around the outer edge of each piece. For the head, be sure to stitch around the cutouts as well, so that you'll be able to see the stitching even after we add the hood piece.

7

7. Stitch the top robe layer and hood. Position the robe top layer and pin in place. Use one strand of black floss to make a running stitch around the outer edge of the piece. Position the hood so that the bottom of the hood overlaps the top of the robe. Use one strand of black floss to make a running stitch around the hood, centering your stitches in the hood piece as you work.

8

8. Add the reaper's face. Position the eyes, nose, and cheeks in the lower two-thirds of the face. Use one strand of coordinating floss (black-brown and light pink) to make a single vertical stitch in each eye, and a single horizontal stitch in each cheek, and two stitches in a "V" shape in the nose. These pieces are too small to pin, so be sure to work slowly and carefully.

9. Stitch the trick-or-treat bucket and scythe base. Position the pumpkin base and scythe handle. Use one strand of coordinating floss (dark orange and dark brown) to make a running stitch around the outer edge of each piece, leaving the bottom edge of the pumpkin bucket unstitched.

9

10. Stitch the scythe blade and add detail. Position the scythe blade and pin it in place. Use one strand of medium-gray floss to make a running stitch around the outer edge of the piece. To add a little bit of detail to the scythe, use one strand of dark-brown floss to stitch several small "X" shapes where the scythe blade meets the handle.

10

11. Add detail to the trick-or-treat bucket. Use a heat-erasable pen to draw a curved horizontal line near the top of the bucket (to create an opening) and four curved vertical lines on the bucket (coming from the points between the bumps along the bottom and extending to that top horizontal line). Use one strand of dark-orange floss to backstitch each of these lines. Use one strand of dark-brown floss to make two French-knot eyes and a fly-stitch mouth on the pumpkin. Fill the top of the bucket with French-knot candies in a variety of colors (magenta, red, dark yellow, and bright green).

11

12. Stitch the cloud and bats. Position the bats and cloud in the sky (the curve of the cloud should align with the upper right edge of the hoop). Pin the cloud in place. Secure each bat by using a single strand of black-brown floss to make a vertical couching stitch in the center of the bat shape. This allows the wings to lift off the hoop and give the illusion of flight! Use one strand of cream floss to make a running stitch around the outer edge of the cloud.

12

working *with* kiddos

- **Allow your child to practice their running stitch.** This piece has a lot of opportunity to practice running stitch on large and simple shapes. The grass, sidewalk, reaper pieces, and bush all allow for plenty of space to practice without having to worry about tight corners or narrow spaces. If your child is feeling confident, let them take the lead on some of the stitching here!

- **Let your child decide on the candy.** While I've given some suggested colors to use for the French-knot candies, your child may have other ideas. Maybe they have another color palette in mind or want the candy to look more like some of their favorites. If so, put them in charge of choosing the colors! They can also decide where to place each color or even stitch the French knots on their own if they're feeling bold.

- **Put your child in charge of the night sky.** There's plenty of room for creativity and customization with the night sky on this piece. More bats? A moon and stars? A spooky, cloudy night? The possibilities are endless, and this would be a fun way to give your child some creative control over the piece. Feel free to use templates from other projects in this book, or even make your own!

If your child feels confident enough to try this project entirely on their own, let them know you're nearby for help if they need it!

cozy campfire

S'mores are a classic camping treat, and for good reason! The combination of gooey marshmallow, melted chocolate, and crispy graham cracker is delicious and really the only thing I like about camping. The smell of a bonfire and the joy of toasting marshmallows while in the company of loved ones are peak cozy vibes—and something I absolutely wanted to bring to this book. Of course, I had to give this experience an adorable kawaii spin, so we have a happy little s'more roasting his own sweet treats at a (maybe slightly magical) campfire.

This pattern brings all the warmth of a campfire with its color palette and so much coziness with its sweet subject matter. A handful of basic stitches and some expert layering bring the whole scene to life.

Templates on page 148.

supplies

- 8" (20 cm) embroidery hoop
- cotton fabric in maroon
- felt in colors shown at right
- 6-strand embroidery floss in colors: medium brown, white, rich brown, dark brown, light brown, black-brown, pink, light yellow, red, orange, dark yellow, bright yellow, medium yellow
- white felt for backing

tools

- embroidery needle
- straight pins
- scissors
- heat-erasable pen
- hot-glue gun

stitches used

- running stitch
- backstitch
- French knot
- fill stitch

felt colors

- hazelnut
- acorn
- nutmeg
- toast
- linen
- tellina
- sesame
- carmine
- tangerine
- golden
- lemonade

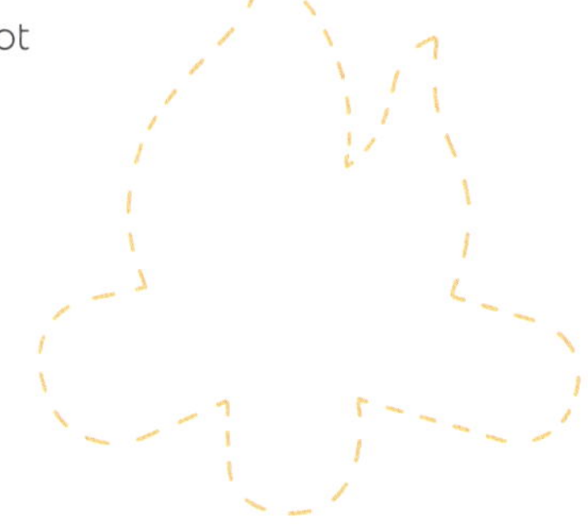

1. Stitch the log bases. To begin, let's set the scene by getting the base pieces in place. Position both log bases toward the bottom of the hoop, with the marshmallow to the left of the campfire. Pin both pieces in place. Use one strand of medium-brown floss to make a running stitch around the outer edge of each piece.

2. Stitch the marshmallow and add the end piece to the log. Let's focus on the marshmallow to start. Position the marshmallow piece and pin in place. Use one strand of white floss to make a running stitch around the outer edge of the piece. Position the log end on the left side of the log. Use one strand of rich-brown floss to make a running stitch around the outer edge of the piece. Use a heat-erasable pen to draw a small spiral on the log end. Use one strand of dark-brown floss to backstitch the spiral.

3. Stitch the chocolate. Position the chocolate piece on top of the marshmallow. Be sure the sides on the marshmallow itself align (it's okay if the top of the chocolate doesn't align perfectly with the top of the marshmallow, because we'll be putting the graham cracker in place). Pin it in place. Use one strand of dark-brown floss to make a running stitch around the outer edge of the piece.

4. Stitch the graham-cracker base layer. We're nearing the end of building the marshmallow buddy! Position the graham-cracker base layer on top of the chocolate layer so that the top edge and corners align with the chocolate. Pin it in place. Use one strand of light-brown floss to make a running stitch around the outer edge of the piece.

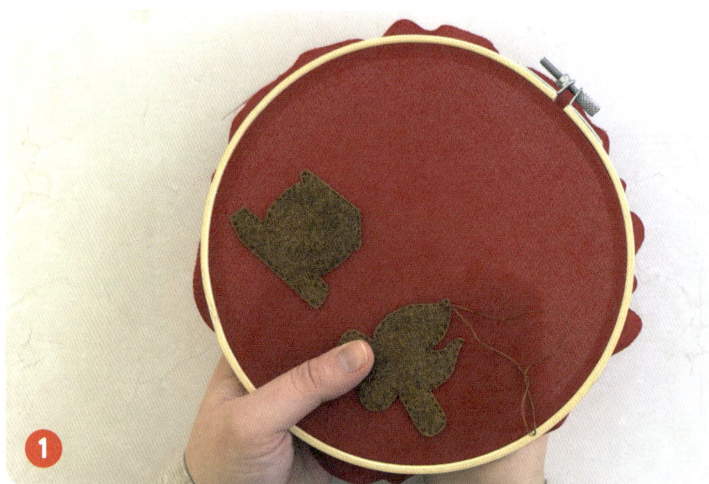
1

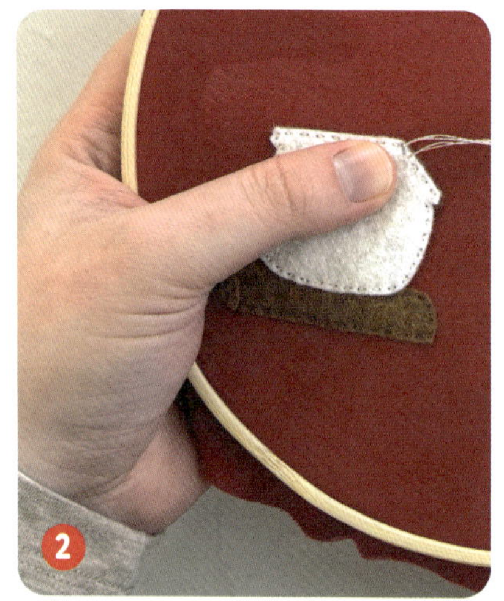
2

3

4

5

6

5. Stitch the graham-cracker top layer. Position the top layer of the graham cracker and pin it in place. Use one strand of light-brown floss to make a running stitch around the outer edge. Make a vertical stitch at the left corner to show that the graham cracker has a top and edges. Make a vertical stitch to cut the graham cracker in half, then add small French knots to each half to make the cracker look even more realistic.

6. Add detail to the marshmallow and stitch the roasting stick. Use a heat-erasable pen to draw arms, legs, a face, and the roasting stick. Use two strands of black-brown floss to make straight stitches for the arms, legs, and roasting stick. Continue using those two strands to make fill-stitch eyes and feet and to backstitch the smile. Use two strands of pink floss to make fill-stitch cheeks. To add the treats to the roasting stick, position them along the length and secure each one with a single vertical stitch in one strand of coordinating floss (pink, light yellow, and white).

7

7. Stitch the top log for the fire. Let's begin work on the fire now that the s'more is all finished! Position the top-log piece so that it overlaps the base layer; this will add a bit of definition for the logs without us having to embroider those lines. Pin the piece in place. Use one strand of medium-brown floss to make a running stitch around the outer edge of the piece.

8

8. Add the log ends to the fire. Position the log ends on their respective logs. Use one strand of rich-brown floss to make a running stitch around the outer edge of each piece. Use a heat-erasable pen to draw a spiral on each of the log ends. Use one strand of dark-brown floss to backstitch each spiral.

9. Stitch the flame base. Now it's time to add some fire! Position the flame base so that it's aligned with the layers beneath it and pin it in place. Use one strand of red floss to make a running stitch around the outer edge of the piece.

10. Stitch the flame center. To finish off the fire, position the flame center so that the bottom edge is just touching the bottom edge of the flame base. Use one strand of orange floss to make a running stitch around the outer edge of the piece.

11. Stitch the sparks. Position your embers around the flame, billowing up toward the sky. Use one strand of coordinating floss (dark yellow, bright yellow, and medium yellow) to secure each spark with either a cross in the middle (for the four-pointed sparks) or a six-pointed star (for the six-pointed sparks). Use a heat-erasable pen to mark out the positions of French knots. Use three strands of floss to stitch each knot, using various shades of yellow to do so.

12. Add the moon and clouds to the sky. Position the moon and clouds in the sky above the s'more and campfire. Pin each piece in place. Use one strand of coordinating floss (white and light yellow) to make a running stitch around the outer edge of each piece to complete the design.

working *with* kiddos

- **Get your child's help with cutting pieces.** While many of the pieces for this design are a bit smaller in scale, they're the perfect chance to practice for more confident or experienced kiddos. They can perfect the art of getting smooth cuts on the curves of the clouds, moon, or flame pieces and can practice some slightly sharper (but not too difficult) corners and turns on the various marshmallow components. You know your child best, so remember it's okay to step in and help if they need it.
- **Allow your child to stitch some of the easier components.** Most of the layers in both the s'more and the campfire are fairly easy to stitch with minimal assistance. While the spirals on the log ends or the detail on the graham cracker may be intimidating, the rest of the pieces lend themselves well to young stitchers. Make your child the primary stitcher for some of these easier elements to boost their crafting confidence.
- **Put your child in charge of the campfire.** When it comes to deciding how many sparks and embers to include around the campfire and where everything should go, there's no one better to consult than your young collaborator. This is the perfect opportunity for them to put their composition skills to work and decide on the layout and colors to use for each spark. They could even experiment with different spark shapes if they feel so inspired!

This project is only listed as a level 2 because some of the pieces are very small. The stitches and layering techniques are very beginner-friendly. If your child feels confident enough to try this project entirely on their own, let them know you're nearby for help if they need it!

haunted forest library

Books have always held a special kind of magic for me. One of my favorites as a kid was *The Secret Garden*, and I spent so much time hoping that I would stumble across my own key to a hidden world that was all my own. I firmly believe that magic is waiting for all of us just around the corner! All these ideas swirled together into this little library. Nestled deep in a moss-covered forest that's probably home to a ghost or two, this library is chock-full of books to help you on your path toward more magic in your life.

This pattern involves some very tiny pieces and intricate vine work, but the stitches aren't anything more complex than you've already done. We'll be relying on those simple embroidery stitches to bring this piece to life in a whole new way.

Templates on pages 149–150.

supplies

- 8" (20 cm) embroidery hoop
- cotton fabric in olive green
- felt in colors shown at right
- 6-strand embroidery floss in colors: dark brown, beige, copper, black-brown, dark red, medium orange, dark green, eggplant, cream, gold, rich brown, dark orange, gray, bright green, light brown, medium green
- white felt for backing

tools

- embroidery needle
- straight pins
- scissors
- heat-erasable pen
- hot-glue gun
- ruler or other straightedge

stitches used

- running stitch
- backstitch
- detached chain stitch
- fly stitch
- French knot
- couching stitch

felt colors

- hazelnut
- cocoa
- umber
- nutmeg
- oyster
- garnet
- Chantenay
- pumpkin
- butterscotch
- bellwether ecru
- nori
- zucchini
- citron
- Malbec
- terrazzo

haunted forest library

1. Stitch the library base layer. Position the library base layer so that the curved edge at the bottom of the post aligns with the bottom edge of your hoop. Pin the piece in place. Use one strand of dark-brown floss to make a running stitch around the outer edge of the piece.

1

2. Add the library box. Position the library box so that the sides and bottom corners align with the base piece. (It's okay if your top edges don't perfectly match up; the roof pieces will cover them.) Pin the piece in place. Use one strand of beige floss to make a running stitch around the outer edge of the piece.

2

3. Stitch the roof and cubby base. Position the roof piece so that the top edge and corners align with the library box and pin it in place. Position the cubby so that it's centered in the visible portion of the library box. Pin the piece in place. Use one strand of coordinating floss (copper and black-brown) to make a running stitch around the outer edge of each piece.

3

4. Stitch the rooftop and cubby frame. Position the rooftop piece and pin it in place. Use one strand of copper floss to make a running stitch around the edge of the piece. Position the cubby frame so that the edges align with the cubby base. This piece is much too narrow to pin, so you'll need to work slowly and carefully. Use one strand of copper floss to make a running stitch around the whole frame, centering your stitches.

4

5. Stitch the book bases and add detail to the roof. Position the book bases and pin each one in place. Use one strand of coordinating floss (dark red, medium orange, dark green, eggplant, and dark brown) to make a running stitch around the edge of each book. To add detail to the roof, use a ruler (or something similar) and a heat-erasable pen to make two straight, horizontal lines (mine are about ½" / 1.3 cm apart). Make staggered vertical lines along the lengths to give the appearance of bricks or shingles. Use one strand of copper floss to make long, straight stitches for each of these lines; the horizontal stitches should run the length of one shingle.

Tip:

For larger eye sockets for your skull, wrap your two strands around your needle three times!

6. Add detail to book 1. Position the skull and bone pieces so that they're centered on the spine of the book. Use one strand of cream floss to make a running stitch around the edge of each piece (I left the bottom edge of the skull unstitched for a cleaner look). Use two strands of black-brown floss to make French-knot eyes and a fly-stitch nose. Use two strands of gold floss to make horizontal couching stitches near the top and bottom of the book's spine.

7. Add detail to book 2. Position the dark-brown rectangles near the top and bottom of the book's spine and use one strand of dark-brown floss to backstitch a rectangle just inside the border of the piece. Position the light-brown rectangles just below or just above the dark-brown pieces and use one strand of rich-brown floss to make a single horizontal stitch in the center of each piece. Use a heat-erasable pen to draw a curved stem on the leaf. Center the leaf on the book spine and use one strand of black-brown floss to backstitch the stem (be sure to extend it past the bottom edge of the leaf a little bit).

8. Add detail to book 3. Position the pumpkins so that they're centered and evenly spaced on the third book spine. Use one strand of dark-orange floss to make a running stitch around the edge of each pumpkin. To create stems, use two strands of dark-brown floss to make several vertical stitches coming from the top of each pumpkin.

9. Add detail to book 4. Position the gray rectangles near the top and bottom of the spine of the book. Use one strand of gray floss to backstitch a rectangle just inside the border of the piece. Center the potion bottle template on the spine and use a heat-erasable pen to trace the outline. Use one strand of gray floss to backstitch the outline. Position the back layer of the potion inside the outline of the bottle and use one strand of dark-green floss to make a running stitch around the edge of the piece. Repeat this process for the bright-green front piece of the potion.

10. Add detail to book 5. Position the light-brown rectangles so that they're aligned with the top and bottom edges of the book's spine. Use one strand of light-brown floss to make a single horizontal stitch in the center of each piece. Position the moon phase pieces so that they're centered and evenly spaced. The full moon should be in the center, the half moons above and below the full moon, and the crescents at the top and bottom. Use one strand of beige floss to make a single horizontal stitch in the center of each crescent and half moon, and to make a running stitch around the outer edge of the full moon.

11. Stitch the cubby knob and add vines to the library. To give the appearance of a glass door protecting the cubby, let's add the doorknob piece. Use one strand of gold floss to make a running stitch around the outer edge of the knob. Use a heat-erasable pen to draw vines curling around the library. Don't worry if yours don't look exactly like mine. Vines are organic and unpredictable! Use two strands of medium-green floss to backstitch the vines, adding in pairs of detached chain leaves along the length; I added leaves to every fourth stitch.

12. Stitch the falling leaves. Scatter the falling leaves around the space outside the library. Use one strand of black-brown floss to backstitch a slightly curved stem for each leaf. You can either use a heat-erasable pen to draw the stems on, or simply freehand them (they're fairly easy to create with three to four stitches).

working *with* kiddos

- **Put your child in charge of the book designs.** The great thing about libraries is that we all have access to a huge variety of different books and get to choose what we're most interested in. That applies to this library as well! Maybe your child would like to design their own book spines to fit into this library. Maybe they want the books in a different order. This is a great opportunity to let their creativity shine!
- **Let your child draw the vines.** For kiddos who might be overwhelmed by the possibilities of book design, but who still want to be part of the design process, the vines are the perfect job. Hand over the heat-erasable pen and let them decide how the vines should be growing in this forest. Just be sure to remind them to use sketching motions rather than dragging the pen, as most of the drawing will be happening on the felt.
- **Allow your child to place and stitch the falling leaves.** The falling leaves are another great opportunity for creative autonomy with this design. Allow your child to determine where the leaves should go and how many to include. If they're feeling confident and empowered, they could even stitch all the stems!

This project is listed as intermediate because it involves a lot of tiny pieces and intricate embroidery work. That said, if your child feels confident enough to try this project entirely on their own, let them know you're nearby for help if they need it!

jolly snowman

Winter is hands down my favorite season. I love the cold weather, the twinkling lights, the cozy nights in with lots of blankets and blustery winds outside, and all the warm beverages and sweet treats that only come around for the season. One of my favorite parts of winter is the snow, especially when there's enough for an afternoon of family snowman construction. For times when there isn't any snow on the ground and you just want the cozy feeling that building a snowman brings, this project is perfect!

This pattern may use just a few basic stitches, but we'll be putting those stitches to work and exploring pattern with this one. While the design itself is simple, those clean lines and a limited color palette allow the bold pattern of the snowman's scarf and the textures of the hat to really have their moment.

Templates on pages 151–152.

supplies

- 8" (20 cm) embroidery hoop
- cotton fabric in blue
- felt in colors shown at right
- 6-strand embroidery floss in colors: white, dark brown, medium orange, light pink, red, black-brown, bright orange
- white felt for backing

tools

- embroidery needle
- straight pins
- scissors
- heat-erasable pen
- hot-glue gun

stitches used

- running stitch
- backstitch
- French knot
- couching stitch

felt colors

- bellwether white
- chicory
- hazelnut
- tellina
- salmon
- rhubarb
- clementine

jolly snowman

1. Stitch the snowbank. Position the snowbank piece so that the bottom curved edge aligns with the bottom edge of your hoop. Pin the piece in place. Use one strand of white floss to make a running stitch around the outer edge of the piece. This piece is flush against the edge of the hoop, so your stitches may not be as close to the edge of the felt when working along the bottom edge, and that's okay!

2. Stitch the snowman base. Let's begin building our snowman! Position the snowman base so that it's centered in the hoop and overlapping with the snowbank by about ½" (1.3 cm). Pin it in place. Use one strand of dark-brown floss to make a running stitch along the outer edge of the piece.

3. Add some snow. Position the snow layer on the snowman and pin it in place. Use one strand of white floss to make a running stitch along the outer edge of the piece. Use a heat-erasable pen to map out snowflakes in the sky. Turn a few of them into six-pointed snowflakes if you like! Use three strands of white floss to make French-knot snowflakes and stitch any six-pointed snowflakes with one strand of white floss.

4. Add the base layers for the hat and scarf. Let's give our snowman some winter gear! Position the base layer for the hat and scarf in the appropriate spots, and pin both in place. Use one strand of coordinating floss (medium orange and light pink) to make a running stitch around the outer edge of each piece.

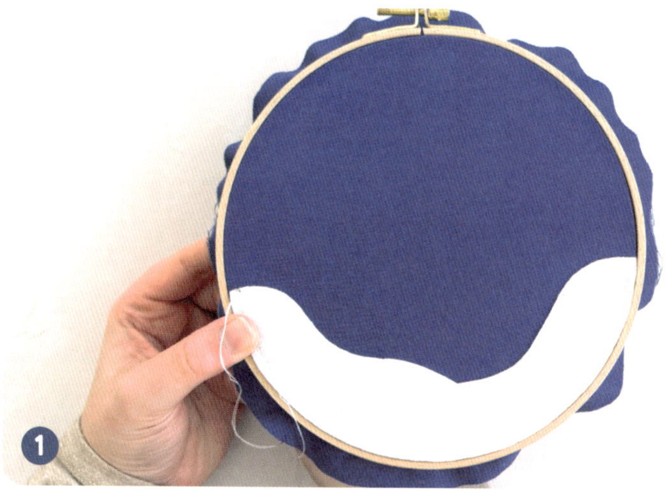
1

2

3

4

5. Add the top layers to the hat and scarf. Position the hat and scarf top layers and pin each of them in place. For the hat, this will include the pom-pom and the hat brim. Use one strand of coordinating floss (red and light pink) to make a running stitch around the outer edge of each piece.

6. Add the face and winter-gear details. Lay out the snowman's face. Use one strand of coordinating floss (black-brown and light pink) to make a single vertical stitch (for the eyes) or horizontal stitch (for the cheeks) in each piece. For the mouth and carrot nose, use one strand of coordinating floss (black-brown and bright orange) to make a running stitch around the outer edge. To add detail to the hat brim, use a heat-erasable pen to make curved vertical lines along the length of the brim, and backstitch each line with one strand of red floss. To add detail to the scarf, use a heat-erasable pen to draw a stripe and zigzag pattern on the top and tail of the scarf. Use two strands of light-pink floss for the zigzags (you can just backstitch the pattern), and two strands of red floss for the stripes. Use two strands of red floss to freehand a fringe by making vertical straight stitches in varying lengths.

Tip:

For some extra texture, add a few little horizontal stitches to the carrot nose!

working *with* kiddos

- **Allow your child to plan out the snowflake placement.** One of the easiest ways to get kiddos involved with patterns that involve organic elements (like snowflakes or stars) is to let them take the reins when it comes to placement. Give them the pen and let them decide if your snowman is standing in a blizzard or a few gentle flurries!
- **Allow your child to take over the running stitch.** With large pieces featuring gentle curves, this is a great time for your kiddo to practice their running stitch on a piece you're creating together. Be prepared for their interest to be short-lived, especially if they're on the younger side, but seeing both of your work in the finished piece will be so special.
- **Give your child creative control with the winter gear.** Hats and scarves are as varied as the people (and snowpeople) who wear them. Maybe your kiddo has a better idea for winter gear patterns (polka dots, stars, hearts, or something else entirely!). Hand over the heat-erasable pen and let their imagination run wild. They could even add a pattern to the hat as well as the scarf.

If your child feels confident enough to try a project entirely on their own, this is a great one to start with!

midnight **magic**

There's something so comforting about being warmly snuggled under a blanket, eating homemade baked goods with a furry friend in your lap, while the air outside chills and the snow gently falls. It's easy to imagine that magical things are happening just outside our windows while we nestle down snug in our beds, and that's exactly the vibe we're bringing to this piece.

This pattern uses layers to show a sleeping cat on a windowsill while their nighttime visitor dashes away outside the window. Don't let the tiny pieces intimidate you! The finished design is truly magical.

Templates on pages 153–154.

supplies

- 8" (20 cm) embroidery hoop
- cotton fabric in tan or cream
- felt in colors shown at right
- 6-strand embroidery floss in colors: navy, dark brown, dark green, white, dark teal, dark orange, cream, copper, black-brown, light pink, dark red, rich brown, gold, tan, bright red
- white felt for backing

tools

- embroidery needle
- straight pins
- scissors
- heat-erasable pen
- chalk pencil
- hot-glue gun

stitches used

- running stitch
- backstitch
- chain stitch
- detached chain stitch
- fly stitch
- French knot

felt colors

- bellwether white
- seaside
- nutmeg
- hazelnut
- tellina
- cherry red
- garnet
- Chantenay
- umber
- bellwether ecru
- evergreen
- viridian
- Orion

1. Stitch the window base. Center the window base and pin it in place. You'll want to leave a bit more space at the bottom to make room for the cat's tail. Use one strand of navy floss to make a running stitch around the outer edge of the piece.

2. Add the window frame. Position the window frame, matching the outer edge of the frame to the outer edge of the base. I used more pins than I normally would and worked slowly so that I could adjust as needed. Use one strand of dark-brown floss to make a running stitch around both the outer and inner edges of the frame.

3. Stitch the tree line and windowsill. Position the tree-line piece along the bottom inner edge of the window frame and pin it in place. Position the windowsill so that it overlaps its place on the window frame and pin in place. Use one strand of coordinating floss (dark green and dark brown) to make a running stitch around the outer edge of each piece. Optional: Use one strand of dark-green floss to make fly-stitch pine needles on the trees.

4. Add snow to the treetops. Position the snow pieces on the tops of the trees. Use one strand of white floss to make a running stitch along the straight edges (leave the curved edges unstitched). Because these pieces are so small, you may wish to just place and stitch one at a time.

1

2

3

4

5. Stitch the cat and gift box base pieces. Position the cat and gift box base layers along the windowsill and pin each of them in place. Use one strand of coordinating floss (dark teal and dark orange) to make a running stitch around the outer edge of each piece. To add a bit of whimsy to your cat, make your running stitches through just the tail piece (rather than stitching it down to the hoop). This gives the cat a uniform appearance while making it possible for the tail to move.

6. Add the cat's head and gift box ribbons. Position the cat's head and pin in place. Use one strand of dark-orange floss to make a running stitch around the outer edge of the head piece. Position the ribbon on the gift box. Use one strand of cream floss to make a running stitch around the outer edge of the ribbon. Because this piece is slim and difficult to pin, you may want to work slowly and stop to check that the ribbon is still straight and centered as you work. Use two strands of cream floss to make a few detached chain ribbon loops on the top of the gift box.

7. Stitch the details on the cat. Position the stripes on the cat's back (the longest stripe should be closest to the head and the shortest closest to the tail). Use one strand of copper floss to make a running stitch around the outer edge of each stripe. Position the nose in the center of the face and stitch with a single horizontal stitch in the center. Use a heat-erasable pen to draw "U" shapes for closed eyes, triangles inside the ears, and three whiskers on each side of the face. Use two strands of black-brown floss to backstitch the eyes and whiskers and two strands of light-pink floss to fill in the triangles in the ears. Position the cheeks below the eyes and use one strand of light-pink floss to make a single horizontal stitch in the center.

8. Stitch the sleigh and reindeer base. Position the reindeer piece along the upper right edge of the window frame and the sleigh at a matching angle in the center of the window frame (it should look like the sleigh is taking off into the sky). Use one strand of coordinating floss (dark red and rich brown) to make a running stitch around the outer edge of each piece. Use a heat-erasable pen to draw a runner under the sleigh (two vertical lines under the sleigh, and a horizontal line that curves up at the front of the sleigh). Use two strands of gold floss to stitch the runner (make straight stitches for the vertical lines, and backstitch the horizontal line).

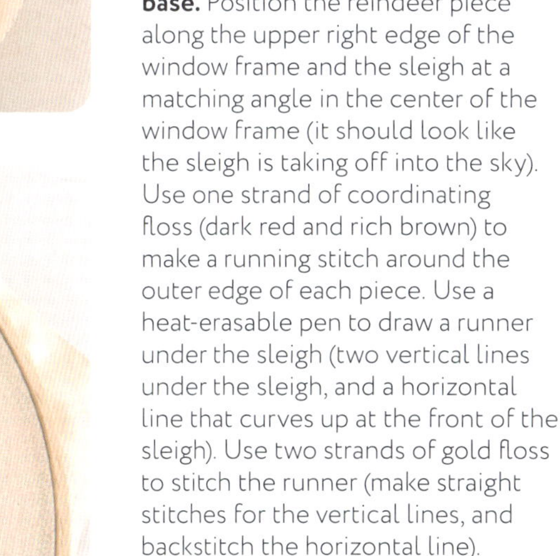

9. Stitch the Santa-base and reindeer-top pieces. Position the Santa-base piece and use one strand of tan floss to make a running stitch around the outer edge. Position the reindeer top piece over the reindeer base. Use one strand of rich-brown floss to stitch around the outer edge.

10. Add the middle layers to Santa and reins to the sleigh. Position the glove and secure with one or two stitches of dark-brown floss. Position the sleeve and use one strand of bright-red floss to make one vertical stitch. Position the hat and use one strand of bright-red floss to make a running stitch around the outer edge. Use a heat-erasable pen to make a horizontal line from the right edge of the reindeer to the center of the sleigh. Use two strands of gold floss to chain-stitch this line. Once finished with the chain stitch, use two strands of gold floss to make a French knot at the sleigh end of the chain.

11. Put the finishing touches on Santa. Use one strand of white floss to make a horizontal stitch in the center of the sleeve cuff. Position the hat brim and use one strand of white floss to make a few horizontal stitches through the center of it. Position the beard and use one strand of white floss to make a running stitch around the outer edge of the beard. Use three strands of tan floss to make a French-knot nose and two strands of black-brown floss to make a French-knot eye. Use three strands of white floss to make three French knots at the pointed end of the hat.

12. Add stars to the sky and lights to the window frame. Use a heat-erasable pen to plot out the position of your stars. Use three strands of white floss to make French-knot stars (you can also add in some six-pointed stars with one strand of white floss if you'd like). Use a heat-erasable pen to draw four curves along the top edge of the window frame. Use two strands of black-brown floss to chain-stitch the light string. Use two strands of white, cream, and gold floss to make French-knot lights along the length of the chain. I placed mine at every other chain, alternating between above and below.

working *with* kiddos

- **Allow your child to practice their running stitch.** While this project does have a lot of very small pieces, the window base (and even the window frame) is the perfect opportunity for your child to practice their running stitch! If they're on a roll and feeling confident, let them keep working on the running stitch for as long as they're interested.
- **Put your child in charge of what's in the night sky.** Maybe your family doesn't celebrate Christmas but still wants to bring a little midnight magic to your space. Allow your child to decide what's in the night sky outside their window. A moon? A spaceship? Something else entirely? Let their imagination run wild and have them help you create templates if needed.
- **Allow your child to choose the colors for the lights above the window.** While I'm a big fan of white/neutral lights, your little helper may have a different vision in mind. Give them free rein to decide what colors to make the little French-knot bulbs (and if they're confident in their French-knot skills, they could even stitch them)!

If your child feels confident enough to try this project entirely on their own, let them know you're nearby for help if they need it!

sweet snow globe

One of my favorite things about winter is something my family likes to call "snow-globe snow." It's that perfect fluffy snow that drifts down gently, the flakes thick and full, with crystal patterns that are visible when they fall on your clothes or hair. It muffles the world and makes it feel like you really are standing in a snow globe, and it never fails to feel like a tiny bit of magic for me.

We'll be capturing some of that magic with this snow-globe design. A cozy little gingerbread house is nestled among the snowdrifts beside a tree with twinkling lights. By using felt that matches our background fabric and some clever chain stitching, we can create the illusion of a clear globe of glass surrounding our scene.

Templates on pages 155–156.

supplies

- 8" (20 cm) embroidery hoop
- cotton fabric in light pink
- felt in colors shown at right
- 6-strand embroidery floss in colors: white, light pink, hot pink, tan, rich brown, dark green, gray, cream, red, light brown, light green
- white felt for backing

tools

- embroidery needle
- straight pins
- scissors
- heat-erasable pen
- hot-glue gun

stitches used

- running stitch
- backstitch
- chain stitch
- detached chain stitch
- French knot
- couching stitch

felt colors

- bellwether white
- seaside
- toast
- nutmeg
- conifer
- wasabi
- rhubarb
- ecru
- peony
- flamingo

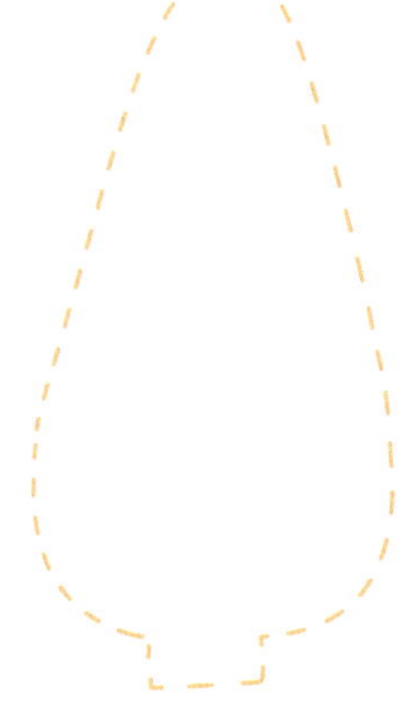

sweet snow globe

1. Stitch the snow-globe base. Center the snow-globe base on the hoop and pin it in place. Use one strand of white floss to make a running stitch around the outer edge of the base piece.

2. Add the snow globe and band. Position the globe piece and the colored band for the pedestal. Pin both pieces in place. Use one strand of coordinating floss (light pink and hot pink) to make a running stitch around the edge of each piece.

3. Add the house base and tree base. Position the house base so that the bottom curve lines up with the bottom of the globe. Pin it in place. The tree should sit to the right of the house, approximately centered between the house and the edge of the globe. Pin the tree as well. Use one strand of coordinating floss (tan and rich brown) to make a running stitch around the edge of each piece.

4. Stitch the lower snowdrift and the treetop. Position the base snowdrift layer and pin it in place. Position the treetop over the tree base and pin it in place as well. Use one strand of coordinating floss (white and dark green) to make a running stitch around the edge of each piece.

5. Add the top snowdrift. Position the top snowdrift and pin it place. Use one strand of white floss to make a running stitch around the outer edge of the snowdrift. By this point, your snow globe should be looking very wintry!

1

2

3

4

5

6. Add details to the tree and colored band. Use a heat-erasable pen to draw swooping, curved lines on your tree. Use two strands of gray floss to chain-stitch each of these curves. Using a mix of cream and the two pinks, make French-knot lights using two strands of floss. For the colored band, use a heat-erasable pen to draw a pattern. I alternated six-pointed snowflakes and French knots, but this is an area to flex your creativity if you have a different idea! Stitch each element using two strands of white floss.

7. Add the chimney top, door, and window base. Because these pieces are quite small and difficult to pin, I recommend working one piece at a time. Position the piece you're working with and hold it in place with your nondominant thumb. Use one strand of coordinating floss (cream, red, and tan) to make a running stitch along the outer edge of each piece.

8. Add the bricks, windowsill, and doorknob. These pieces are even smaller than those in the previous step, so exercise extra care. Use one strand of light-brown floss to make straight stitches along the edges of the bricks and windowsill (your stitches should be a millimeter or two inside the shape). Use one strand of white floss to make a single vertical stitch in the center of the doorknob.

9. Add snow to the gingerbread house. Working one piece at a time, position the snow on the rooftop, chimney top, and windowsill. Use one strand of white floss to make a running stitch around the outer edge of the rooftop piece. Stitch only along the top for the chimney piece and windowsill piece.

10. Add the wreath, candy canes, and curtains. To stitch the curtains, use one strand of light-green floss to make a running stitch along the straight edges of the curtain (leave the curved edge unstitched). Make a single couching stitch at the indent of the curtains to resemble a curtain tie. Repeat for both curtains. To stitch the candy canes, use two strands of red floss to make angled couching stitches along the length of each candy cane. (You may wish to mark out the spacing with a heat-erasable pen before you begin to stitch.) The candy canes should create a heart shape when stitched in place. To stitch the wreath, use one strand of light-green floss to make a running stitch through the center of the circle. Use two strands of white floss to make a detached chain bow (you can stitch the ribbon tails with two to three backstitches per tail). Use two strands of red floss to make a few French-knot berries on the wreath.

11. Add snowflakes to the snow globe. Use a heat-erasable pen to mark out where to put snowflakes on the pink background of the snow globe. Use three strands of white floss to stitch each French-knot snowflake.

12. Chain-stitch around the globe. To complete the illusion of clear glass, create a chain-stitch border around the snow globe. Use two strands of gray floss to make your chain stitch, making sure to nestle your chains right up against the edge of the globe itself. I find the line looks cleanest by beginning at the bottom of the snow globe and working in a counterclockwise direction.

working *with* kiddos

- **Allow your child some design input.** There are a few steps here that involve using a heat-erasable pen to add details to the snow globe. Asking your child's input on the design for the colored band (or letting them draw it on their own), letting them decide on the placement of the lights on the tree, or letting them decide on snowflake placement are perfect low-stress ways to include them in the project.
- **Allow your child to practice their running stitch.** This pattern has some teeny-tiny pieces and details, but it also has some larger pieces that offer a large space to get comfortable with running stitch. If you're making this a collaborative project, letting your child handle the running stitches for the larger pieces is a perfect way to include them in the project.
- **Put your child in charge of the chain stitch from step 12.** Chain stitch may seem intimidating, as it requires two hands, but this pattern is actually the perfect one to practice with! Following the curve of a very large circle is a great guide for practicing this stitch, which is an important one to know if your child is interested in pursuing embroidery further. Demo a few stitches to get them started, then let them complete the chain!

If your child feels confident enough to try this project entirely on their own, let them know you're nearby for help if they need it!

happy little tree farm

Tree farms are such a fun place to visit in the colder months. The crisp smell of pine needles, the crunch of snow beneath your feet, and cups of warm apple cider in your hands all combine to create the perfect seasonal atmosphere. I love bringing life to buildings and structures in my designs, and I knew immediately that a happy little barn surrounded by trees, snow, and stars needed to end up in this book.

With this design, we'll be exploring fabric layering. This technique is excellent for bringing different colors to your background without adding the bulk of a felt layer, but it can sometimes be tricky to master. Luckily, it doesn't matter if your fabric layer ends up perfectly straight, because we'll be covering it with a cute little barn and some gorgeous trees, so this is a great opportunity to experiment.

Templates on page 157.

supplies

- 8" (20 cm) embroidery hoop
- cotton fabric in navy blue and white
- felt in colors shown at right
- 6-strand embroidery floss in colors: white, dark brown, rich brown, light brown, dark red, dark green, bright red, black-brown, light pink
- quilt batting (optional to add padding)
- white felt for backing

tools

- embroidery needle
- straight pins
- scissors
- heat-erasable pen
- chalk pencil
- hot-glue gun

stitches used

- running stitch
- backstitch
- French knot
- fill stitch
- couching stitch

felt colors

- bellwether white
- toast
- hazelnut
- garnet
- tellina
- conifer
- willow
- wasabi

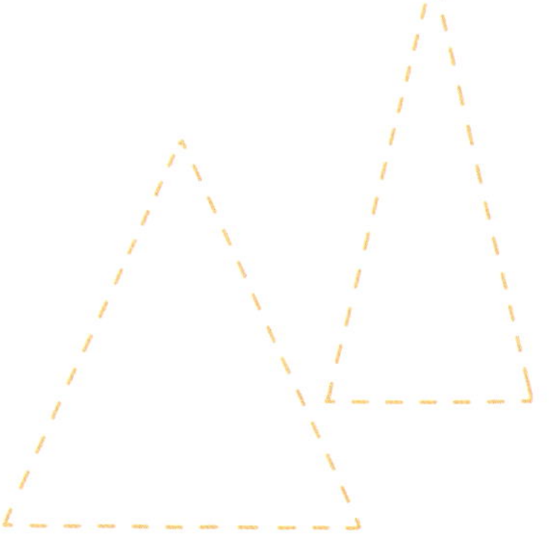

happy little tree farm

1. Prepare your fabric layer and tree pieces. Cut a 10" x 10" (25 x 25 cm) piece each of navy and white fabric. Fold the white fabric in half. Prep your hoop according to the instructions on page 20, but when laying your fabric over the inner hoop, place first your navy fabric and then the white, making sure the folded edge is at the top and the white fabric covers the lower half of the navy fabric (it doesn't have to be exactly half). Finish prepping your hoop as usual. Lay out your trees and use a heat-erasable pen to mark the curves of the hoop if any of them overlap. Trim the excess.

1

Tip:

One of the trickiest parts of fabric layering is pulling your fabric tight while tightening the hoop, as the layers can shift. Work slowly, and don't worry about getting that top layer perfect until you have the top edge stitched down!

2. Secure the white fabric layer. Pin the white fabric layer in place. Use one strand of white floss to make a running stitch along the upper folded edge. Once that top edge is stitched, smooth any wrinkles by gently tugging the fabric overhang outside your hoop. If you need to make some minor adjustments and tighten your hoop further, now is the time to do that.

2

3

3. Stitch the trees. Position the trees where you want them (feel free to lay out your path and barn pieces to make sure your trees look as full and lush as you want them to). I did three trees on one side and five on the other. Stitch each tree with a single vertical stitch from just below the top point to just above the bottom edge. This will allow your trees more movement (and less lumpiness from the overlapping layers). I recommend using two strands of dark brown, rich brown, or light brown, depending on the shade of green for your tree.

4. Stitch the barn base and path. Position the path and barn-base pieces. With all the trees creating uneven layers beneath the barn edges, this may be a place where

4

you want to use some padding. If you'd like to, cut a layer of quilt batting approximately the same shape as the barn (slightly smaller so you don't have fluff sticking out around the edges). Pin the path and barn base with padding underneath. Use one strand of coordinating floss (dark red and light brown) to make a running stitch around the outer edge of each piece.

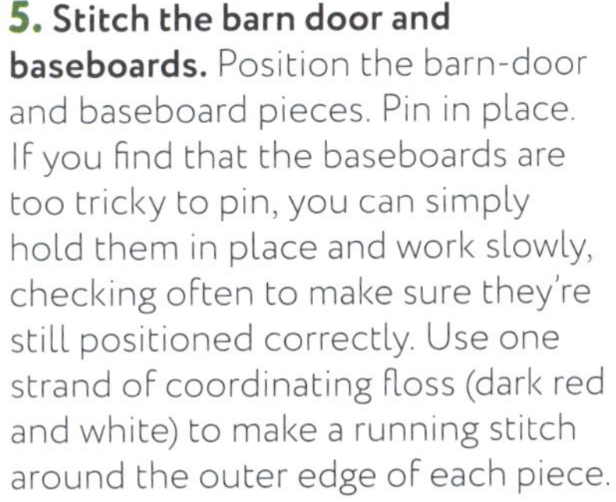

5. Stitch the barn door and baseboards. Position the barn-door and baseboard pieces. Pin in place. If you find that the baseboards are too tricky to pin, you can simply hold them in place and work slowly, checking often to make sure they're still positioned correctly. Use one strand of coordinating floss (dark red and white) to make a running stitch around the outer edge of each piece.

6. Add details to the barn door and baseboards. Use a heat-erasable pen to mark out the borders of the barn door. Use two strands of white floss to backstitch these borders, making sure to create two doors with a top and bottom half. Continue using those two strands of white floss to stitch an "X" shape in each of the four quadrants. Use a heat-erasable pen to mark out placement of the vertical lines for the baseboards. I only marked the top point for each line and then just made sure the floss was lying straight before bringing my needle back down. Stitch these detail lines with one strand of white floss and couching stitches.

7. Stitch the rooftop and window frames. Position the white rooftop piece along the top edge of the barn base. This piece is too narrow to pin, so you'll need to work slowly to make sure the piece is staying properly aligned. Use one strand of white floss to make a running stitch along the edges of the piece. Position the window frames to the left and right of the barn doors. Use one strand of white floss to make a running stitch around each window frame, centering your stitches rather than sticking to one edge. Use two strands of white floss to create an "X" shape inside each window.

8. Add the wreath. Position the wreath in the top half of the barn, centering it in the space. Use one strand of dark-green floss to make a running stitch along both the inner and outer edges of the wreath. Use a heat-erasable pen to mark out where to place berries, then use two strands of bright-red floss to stitch each one with a French knot.

9. Add detail to the barn. Use two strands of white floss to make a single horizontal line across the barn face, from corner to corner (see photo for placement). Use a heat-erasable pen to mark out a smile centered over the barn door, and mark out eyes to the left and right of the smile. Use two strands of black-brown floss to backstitch the smile and stitch each eye with a fill stitch. Position the cheeks below the eyes and secure them with one single horizontal stitch using one strand of light-pink floss.

9

10. Stitch the fence base. Position the fence base so that the curved edges align with the bottom right edge of the hoop. Use one strand of dark-brown floss to make straight stitches along the length of each section of the fence, centering the stitches within the felt. Because this piece is too narrow to pin, you'll want to work slowly and check the alignment frequently.

10

11

11. Stitch the second and third fence layers. Position the second fence layer so that it aligns with the first layer. Use one strand of dark-brown floss to make straight stitches for each fence post and horizontal beam. For longer sections, you may wish to stitch a small tacking stitch at each end of the beam and in the center, before stitching the long single stitch over the top of them. This keeps the felt secure while also giving your fence a seamless look. Repeat this process for the two fence posts.

12. Add stars to the sky. Use a chalk pencil to mark out the placement of stars in the sky. You can turn some of them into six-pointed stars if you want or keep them all as small dots. Stitch any six-pointed stars with one strand of white floss and the French-knot stars with three strands of white floss.

12

working *with* kiddos

- **Put your child in charge of the trees.** How many trees will be on your tree farm? What sizes will they be? This is a great way to get kids involved in this project, especially if their attention span is limited and they only want to contribute for a short time. All the trees are triangle shapes, and while there are templates included, feel free to make your own as well. The beauty of tree farms is that no two trees are exactly alike, and that variety will add an organic feel to your piece.
- **Allow your child to stitch some of the easier components.** Stitching down trees with a single vertical stitch is certainly something even the youngest stitchers can manage on their own. The barn is a nice, big shape and perfect for getting some running-stitch practice in. Make your child the primary stitcher for some of these easier elements to boost their crafting confidence.
- **Give your child creative freedom when it comes to decorating elements.** Maybe your little helper wants something other than a wreath gracing the barn or has a creative vision for the snowy landscape in front of the barn (snowman, anyone?). Let them take the lead when it comes to decorating the tree farm! Maybe they even want to add strings of lights to make the design even more festive. The sky is the limit here!

This project is listed as intermediate because fabric layering can be a bit tricky and the fence is a more intricate piece to put together. However, even with that designation, most of the stitching is fairly easy. If your child feels confident enough to try this project entirely on their own, let them know you're nearby for help if they need it!

3

LEVELING UP YOUR WORK

Now that you've completed a project or two (or maybe all sixteen), you might be wondering what's next. The following pages will show you how to level up your work. There are tips for adding dimension to your pieces, building your own color palettes, creating visual interest (should you branch out and try your hand at designing), and closing and displaying your hoops. I hope that all the skills you've learned and the projects you've tried empower you to branch out and try new things!

Adding Dimension

One of my favorite things about felt appliqué as a medium is all the texture and depth you can bring to a piece by utilizing felt. It really makes it feel like your subject is a living, breathing element ready to jump right out of the hoop, and I always get so excited to see the final result once a project has come together. I've experimented with a lot of different methods to add depth and dimension to felt appliqué pieces and, at this point in my career, have a few tried-and-true techniques that I regularly fall back on. To save you the years of trial and error that I went through, let's look at three of my favorite methods and the situations they suit best!

Adding Dimension with Felt Layers

This is by far my favorite technique to use when designing pieces. When I first started creating felt appliqué pieces, I would design my templates so that they just overlapped very slightly but were basically all one layer. This created pieces that had strange ridges where pieces overlapped, and that can ruin the look you're trying to achieve.

At this stage in my creative journey, I much prefer to build my pieces from the bottom up, working with multiple layers to create more-realistic figures and design elements. You'll notice this often in the patterns included in this book; we begin with a base piece and then layer on smaller and smaller pieces in different colors to create characters and scenery. If you go forward and design your own pieces, I encourage you to treat your design as a puzzle and create your templates with this layering technique in mind.

Adding Dimension with Air

Sometimes when stitching a design, there will be pieces that overlap just slightly, or pieces that you want to lift up or pad just the tiniest bit. For example, I designed a piece with a character holding a bunch of balloons, and while I didn't want to pad every single balloon, I did want them to look full and slightly rounded. This is the perfect scenario for the air technique: times when you want your felt pieces to lift off the hoop just the tiniest bit, without going to the extra effort to add any sort of padding. Here are the steps to achieve this look.

1. **Start by leaving a gap.** Stitch your piece with a running stitch as normal, stopping when you have about ½" (1.3 cm) left to stitch. This technique works best on pieces that are at least 1" (2.5 cm) wide in at least one direction.

2. **Create the air pocket.** Slide your needle under the felt piece and gently lift it up from the base fabric. This creates a little air pocket under the felt, giving it the lift we want!

3. **Finish stitching.** Stitch the remainder of the piece down as normal. Keep your stitches gentle (rather than pulling your floss very tight) to avoid crushing that air pocket.

Adding Dimension with Quilt Batting

In some of my earlier pieces, I would occasionally add fiberfill stuffing under felt when I wanted to add dimension to a design. The problem with fiberfill is that it expands to fill space, so the felt will be very round rather than being a thick but flat layer. In some cases, such as with things like bushes, noses, balloons, etc., this round look is perfectly fine (and maybe even desirable). But most of the time, we want depth and dimension while still maintaining a smooth, flat surface. Enter quilt batting. Soft and fluffy like fiberfill, it's designed to go between quilt panels and thus maintains a flatter surface when layered beneath felt. Here are the steps to utilize this technique.

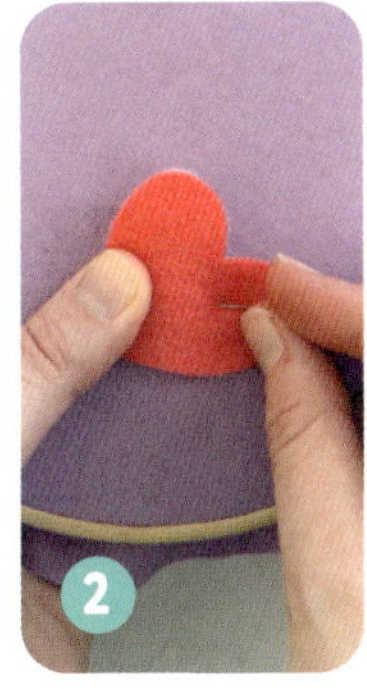
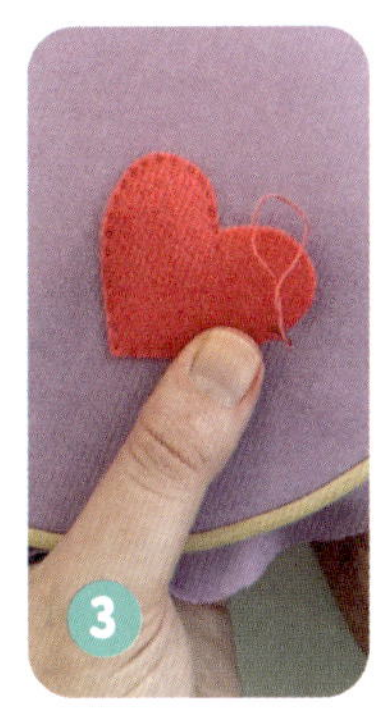

1. **Cut the batting.** Trim a piece of quilt batting to the same shape as your felt piece. I find it works best to make the batting shape slightly smaller than the felt shape, so that none of the fibers are visible once the piece is stitched down.

2. **Place the felt and batting.** Position both pieces in place on your hoop, layering the batting first and then the felt shape on top. If your piece is large enough to pin, you can do so once the pieces are in position. Personally, if the piece is less than 1"–2" (2.5–5 cm) wide, I simply hold it in place with my nondominant thumb while stitching.

3. **Stitch it down.** Secure your felt piece with a running stitch like normal. You can add embroidery embellishments if desired once the piece is stitched down.

Building Color Palettes

Whether you're designing your own piece or reworking one of the designs in this book, knowing color theory and how to put together cohesive and striking color palettes is an important skill to have. I did take a color theory class in college (and loved it), but you don't need to have an extensive background in color theory or design to put together gorgeous palettes! Let's take a look at a few of the most common harmonious color families and how you can choose colors to fit the vibe you're going for.

Common Palettes

Monochromatic

A monochromatic palette features different shades of the same color. For example, in the Make a Wish design (page 34), the various blacks and grays allow the bright-yellow shooting star to really stand out in the scene. The Magical Mushroom Terrarium pattern (page 78) also features a monochromatic palette in shades of brown, which allows the red of the mushroom and the green of the moss to shine.

Analogous

Analogous colors can be found next to each other on the color wheel. For example, the Let's Taco 'Bout It pattern (page 72) uses shades of yellow and orange to create color harmony, and the contrasting teal of the background fabric allows those colors to really shine. The Cozy Campfire design (page 88) also uses an analogous palette but takes it one step further by including the background fabric in that analogous grouping to create a cozy and cohesive look.

Complementary

Complementary colors sit directly opposite each other on the color wheel. Think options like red and green, a classic combination that you've probably seen in numerous settings in your daily life. Blue and orange is another complementary pair, and it features in the Under the Sea pattern (page 56). Complementary colors are very pleasing to our eyes and allow for vibrant and dynamic pieces.

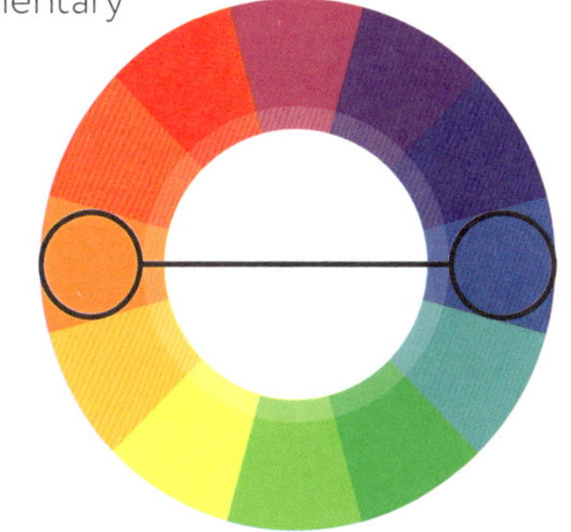

Triadic

Triadic color palettes consist of three colors spaced equally from each other on the color wheel. This type of palette works best when you have a color and want to find accent colors that will play nicely with it. I utilized a triadic palette with the Merry Mermaid pattern (page 66). I had already chosen the coral pink and teal for the mermaid herself, and since yellow is equidistant from those two colors on the color wheel, it ended up being the perfect choice for the fish swimming toward her!

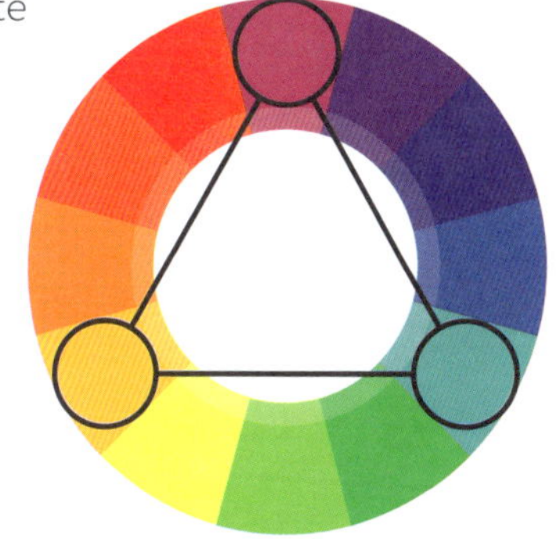

Choosing Background Fabrics

Choosing background fabrics is just as important as choosing your felt palette! The background color you're stitching on helps add to the scene, and you'll want to choose different colors for different purposes. If you're looking for a color to help your subject stand out, consider a complementary or triadic color that provides high contrast for your felt palette. If you're looking for a color that will blend seamlessly into your scene, you may want something that's more monochromatic or analogous in relation to your felt palette.

Closing and Displaying Hoops

You've finished your project! Now what? There are numerous ways to close and display hoops once you're finished stitching. Every artist has their preferred method for closing hoops, some of which include a running stitch around the fabric to cinch it tight in the back, using a cardboard or wooden disc to press the excess fabric down and keep it snug in the hoop, or gluing a circle of felt or paper to the hoop itself or the back of the base fabric. Let's explore our options!

My Preferred Closing Method

Here's my favorite method, which I like for its brevity and great results.

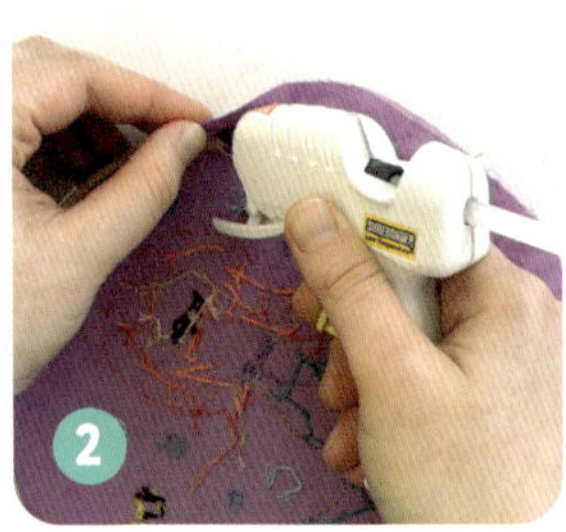

1. Erase guidelines. Use a hairdryer to erase any guidelines you made on your project as you worked. You could also use a small iron as your heat source, but I recommend avoiding an iron if you used acrylic felt, as the iron may melt your felt.

2. Glue it down. Run a thin line of hot glue between the fabric and the hoop. Because hot glue dries quickly, you'll want to do a small section (2"–3"/ 5–7.5 cm) at a time, pulling your fabric tight and then sealing it as you go.

3. Add a felt backing. Cut a 9" x 9" (23 x 23 cm) square of felt and lay it over the back of your hoop. Run a thin line of glue between the felt and the outer hoop. Work in small sections of 2"–3" (5–7.5 cm) all the way around the hoop. As you get closer to the end, begin to gently pull the felt taut as you seal, to keep the back nice and smooth.

4. Trim off excess. Using a small pair of scissors, trim off any excess felt around the edge of the hoop. You can cut the felt down to a circle before gluing it to the back of the hoop, but I prefer to trim it after so that I can make sure it is nice and tight as I'm gluing.

Other Closing Options

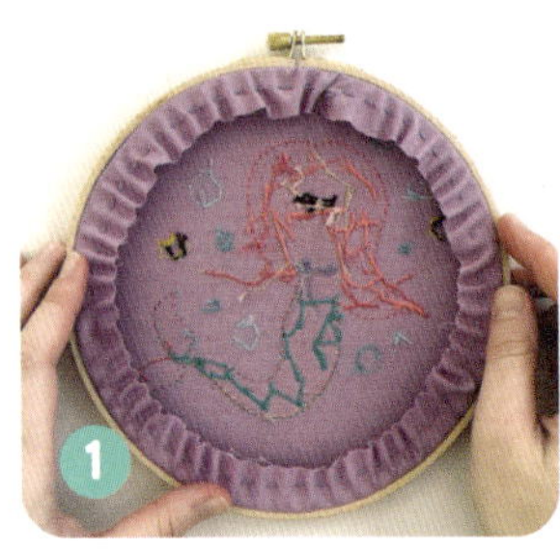

Option 1: Cinching. Pull your fabric taut in your hoop. Thread your needle with one or two strands of a floss that coordinates with your base fabric. Use this floss to make a running stitch about ½" (1.3 cm) from the edge of your fabric. Be sure to gently cinch your fabric (gathering it into a smaller circle) as you work to avoid straining your floss. Once you reach your starting point, trim your floss near the eye of your needle. Gently pull tight and knot the floss.

Option 2: Cardboard. Pull your fabric taut in your hoop. Cut a circle from thick cardboard the diameter of your inner hoop. This piece of cardboard should fit snugly inside your hoop in order to hold your excess fabric as tightly as possible. Fold the excess fabric down around the inner hoop and gently press the cardboard circle down over the fabric. There are also online shops that sell wooden discs for this purpose, if you feel like splurging on them.

Option 3: Combo. This method is a combination of all three methods previously mentioned. Cut a piece of felt the diameter of your inner hoop. Use a thin line of hot glue or fabric glue around the outer edge to glue it to the back of your work (fabric glue will be less likely to show through the front of the hoop). Thread your needle with one or two strands of a coordinating floss, and running stitch around the edge of your excess fabric. Gently cinch your fabric as you work and tie off the floss once you reach your starting point.

Hoop Display Options

There are so many ways to display hoops once they're finished! It all depends on what you want to bring to your space. Here are a few of my favorite options.

1. Hang on the Wall. This is how I display most of my hoops in my own home, and it really brings an element of rustic charm. Be sure to place your nail at an angle and leave about ½" (1.3 cm) protruding from the wall so that the hoop will lie flush.

2. Painted Hoop. If you're looking to bring in a bit more color or want the hoop to be less noticeable so that the piece appears more seamless, you can paint your hoop! I recommend letting the paint cure for 24 hours before beginning your project. Most wooden and bamboo hoops take acrylic paint really well, and you can even use Posca paint pens for more precision with your painting! Paint pens will also eliminate any visible brushstrokes that might come from using a paintbrush.

3. Hoop Frame. If you're looking for a more elegant way to display your hoops, you can invest in hoop frames. Kate from Modern Hoopla makes the most beautiful frames in a variety of shapes and finishes. These are wonderful because they don't require any additional steps for the framing process. Simply pop your hoop into the frame and display!

4. Hoop Easel or Stand. If you're looking to display your hoop on a shelf or surface instead of hanging it on a wall, easels or hoop stands are a great option. They come in a variety of styles and finishes and can be purchased at many art supply stores. Modern Hoopla also carries a few different options if you're looking for stands instead of frames. These offer a little cradle for your hoop to rest in and are also very easy to set up.

Floss Color Guide

Here are the DMC floss colors that I used for each project, if you're interested in matching your colors to mine exactly—but you have total creative control and can adapt colors to suit your needs and floss stash! Note that I used generic names for the colors that made sense in the context of the individual projects—so, for example, I might call one single shade "light green" in one project but "medium green" in another, depending on the variety and number of different greens used in each project. Refer only to the project you're working on to get the correct color references!

Shooting-Star Sampler

Black: 310
Gray: 762
Pink: 602
Orange: 741
Yellow: 725
Green: 907
Blue: 964

Make a Wish

Light yellow: 10
Dark yellow: 3821
Light gray: 762
Medium gray: 415
Dark gray: 318
Black: 310
Pink: 3716

Buddies in Bloom

Dark brown: 801
Copper: 400
Dark green: 904
Light green: 581
Dark pink: 335
Light pink: 3326
White: 3865
Light yellow: 10
Black: 310
Dark yellow: 3821

Fast-Food Friends

Dark brown: 801
Gold: 783
Bright red: 817
Green: 581
Light brown: 436
Black-brown: 3371
Cream: 712
Pale yellow: 3822
White: 3865
Bright yellow: 444
Magenta: 3804

Beam Me Up

Light yellow: 10
Light gray: 928
Pale purple: 25
Dark gray: 169
Light purple: 210
Medium purple: 30
Black: 310
Dark purple: 550
Dusty purple: 3836
Dark teal: 3808
Medium teal: 3809
Medium yellow: 3821
Dark pink: 3803
Dusty rose: 3727
Light peach: 3774
Light orange: 951
Light pink: 225

Under the Sea

Light blue: 964
Dark blue: 3849
Black: 310
Peach: 951
Light orange: 3856
Medium orange: 352
Greenish-blue: 3813

Serene Shore

Dark blue: 3809
Light green: 3364
White: 3865
Red: 817
Dark green: 904
Copper: 400
Light brown: 436
Black-brown: 3371
Beige: 842
Light yellow: 677
Light pink: 225
Light blue: 3849

Merry Mermaid

Dark pink: 335
Tan: 3864
Light purple: 3042
Dark teal: 943
Medium teal: 3851
Coral: 3706
Black-brown: 3371
Light pink: 761
Dark purple: 30
Yellow: 444
Medium blue: 3849
Light blue: 964

Let's Taco 'Bout It

Dark orange: 741
White: 3865
Dark brown: 801
Light orange: 3856
Medium green: 581
Dark yellow: 972
Cream: 677
Black: 310
Red: 666
Dark pink: 3706
Medium pink: 761
Medium yellow: 3821
Gray: 928
Beige: 738
Black-brown: 3371

Magical Mushroom Terrarium

Beige: 842
Cream: 712
Red: 3777
Green: 730
Dark brown: 801
Black-brown: 3371
Pink: 761
Gray: 648
Yellow: 677

Trick or Treat

Medium green: 936
Medium gray: 648
Dark gray: 07
Blue-gray: 413
Dark green: 3345
Light yellow: 677
Black: 310
Cream: 712
Black-brown: 3371
Light pink: 225
Dark orange: 3776
Dark brown: 801
Magenta: 917
Red: 666
Dark yellow: 972
Bright green: 581

Cozy Campfire

Medium brown: 869
White: 3866
Rich brown: 434
Dark brown: 801
Light brown: 436
Black-brown: 3371
Pink: 761
Light yellow: 677
Red: 666
Orange: 741
Dark yellow: 972
Bright yellow: 444
Medium yellow: 727

Haunted Forest Library

Dark brown: 801
Beige: 842
Copper: 400
Black-brown: 3371
Dark red: 3777
Medium orange: 976
Dark green: 936
Eggplant: 35
Cream: 712
Gold: 783
Rich brown: 434
Dark orange: 3776
Gray: 648
Bright green: 581
Light brown: 840
Medium green: 471

Jolly Snowman

White: 3865
Dark brown: 801
Medium orange: 352
Light pink: 761
Red: 3705
Black-brown: 3371
Bright orange: 971

Midnight Magic

Navy: 823
Dark brown: 801
Dark green: 890
White: 3865
Dark teal: 3808
Dark orange: 3776
Cream: 712
Copper: 400
Black-brown: 3371
Light pink: 761
Dark red: 3777
Rich brown: 434
Gold: 3852
Tan: 3864
Bright red: 817

Sweet Snow Globe

White: 3865
Light pink: 963
Hot pink: 603
Tan: 3864
Rich brown: 434
Dark green: 904
Gray: 762
Cream: 746
Red: 3705
Light brown: 436
Light green: 3364

Happy Little Tree Farm

White: 3865
Dark brown: 801
Rich brown: 434
Light brown: 436
Dark red: 3777
Dark green: 904
Bright red: 817
Black-brown: 3371
Light pink: 761

4

TEMPLATES

In this section you'll find all the templates for every piece of every project in this book. They are on perforated pages to make them easy to pull out of the book. I recommend photocopying them so you don't lose the originals (or the templates on the backside of whatever page you're using). You also have the option to download a PDF of all the templates to print whatever you need (link below). All templates are presented at 100% real size to make them super convenient! Time to get tracing and cutting.

Download these templates!

Download all the appliqué patterns featured in this book at www.betterdaybooks.com/felt-craft-fun-pattern-download

Mouth
Cut 1 (black)
Star
Cut 1 (parchment)
Pattern for tracing

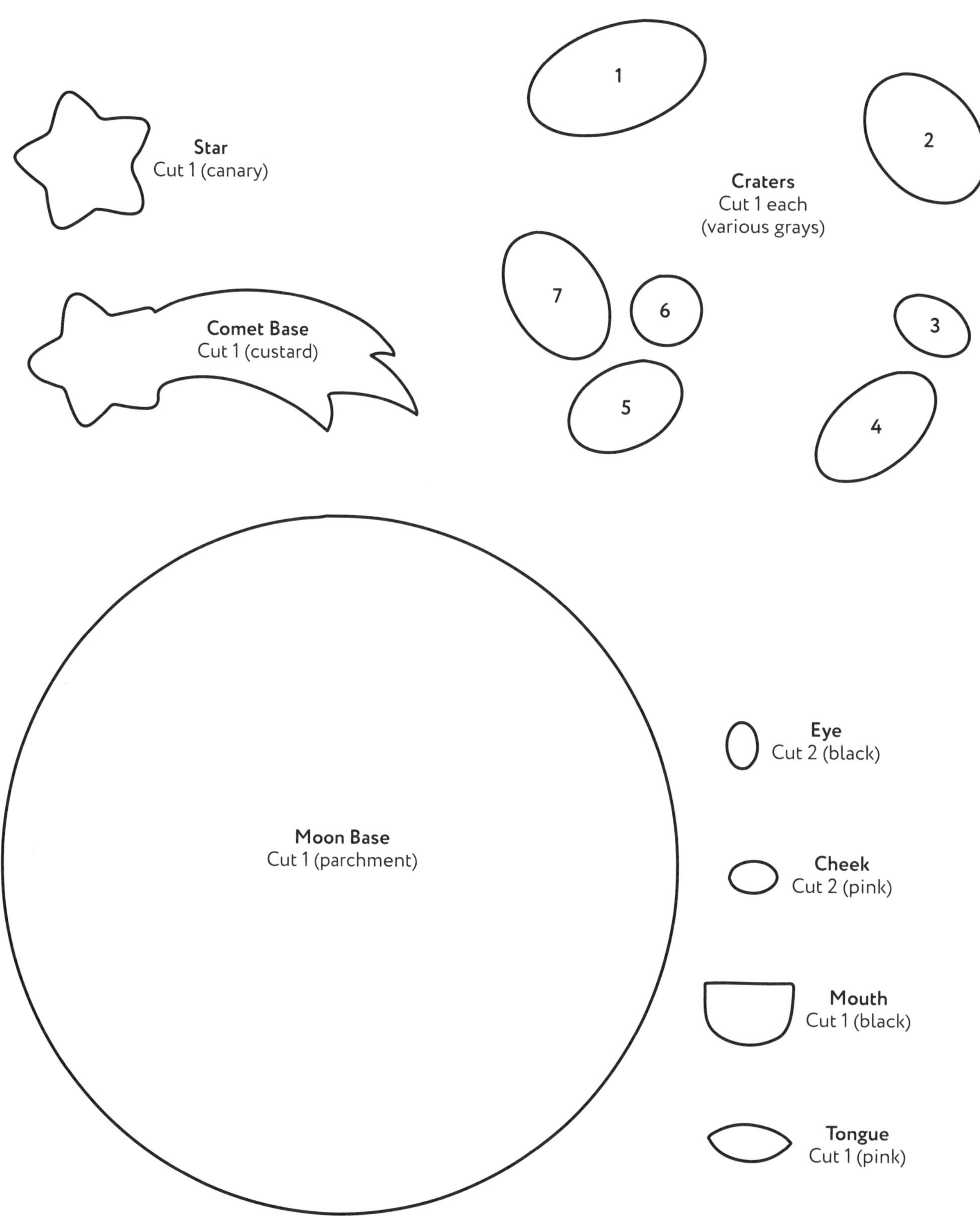

Star
Cut 1 (canary)
Comet Base
Cut 1 (custard)
1
2
Craters
Cut 1 each
(various grays)
7
6
3
5
4
Moon Base
Cut 1 (parchment)
Eye
Cut 2 (black)
Cheek
Cut 2 (pink)
Mouth
Cut 1 (black)
Tongue
Cut 1 (pink)

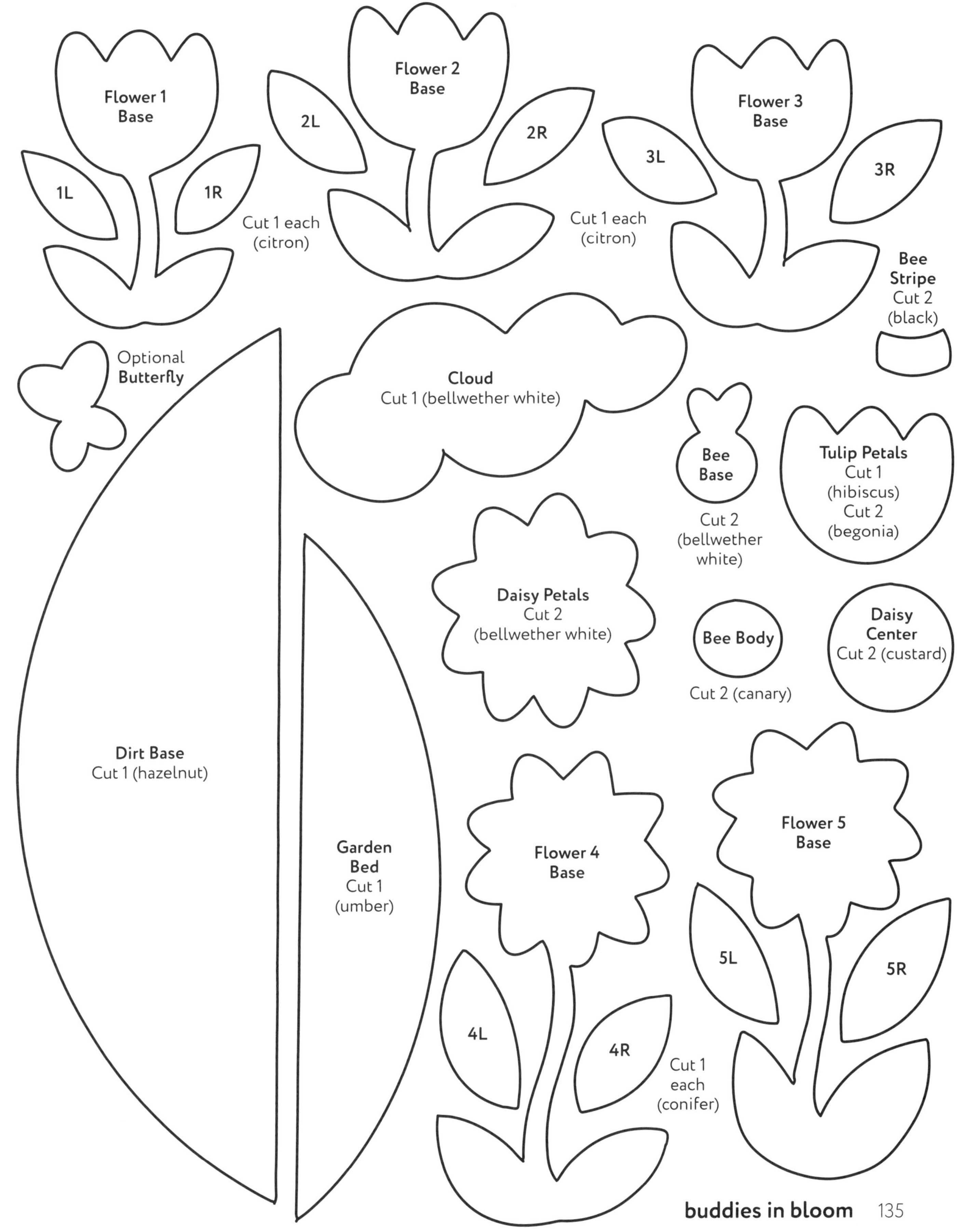
Flower 1 Base
1L
1R
Flower 2 Base
2L
2R
Cut 1 each (citron)
Flower 3 Base
3L
3R
Cut 1 each (citron)
Bee Stripe Cut 2 (black)
Optional Butterfly
Cloud Cut 1 (bellwether white)
Bee Base
Cut 2 (bellwether white)
Tulip Petals Cut 1 (hibiscus) Cut 2 (begonia)
Daisy Petals Cut 2 (bellwether white)
Bee Body
Cut 2 (canary)
Daisy Center Cut 2 (custard)
Dirt Base Cut 1 (hazelnut)
Garden Bed Cut 1 (umber)
Flower 4 Base
4L
4R
Cut 1 each (conifer)
Flower 5 Base
5L
5R

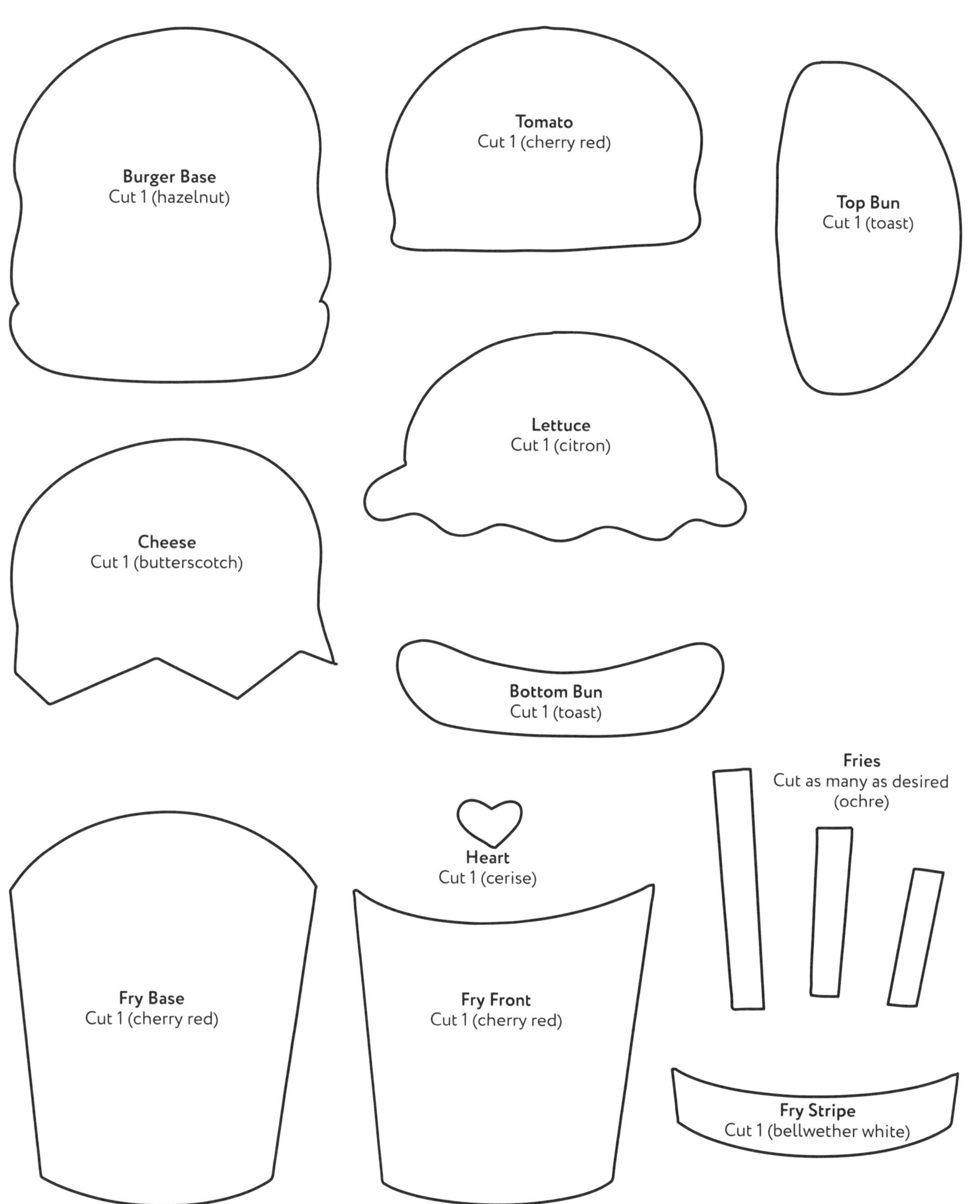
Burger Base
Cut 1 (hazelnut)
Tomato
Cut 1 (cherry red)
Top Bun
Cut 1 (toast)
Lettuce
Cut 1 (citron)
Cheese
Cut 1 (butterscotch)
Bottom Bun
Cut 1 (toast)
Fries
Cut as many as desired
(ochre)
Heart
Cut 1 (cerise)
Fry Base
Cut 1 (cherry red)
Fry Front
Cut 1 (cherry red)
Fry Stripe
Cut 1 (bellwether white)

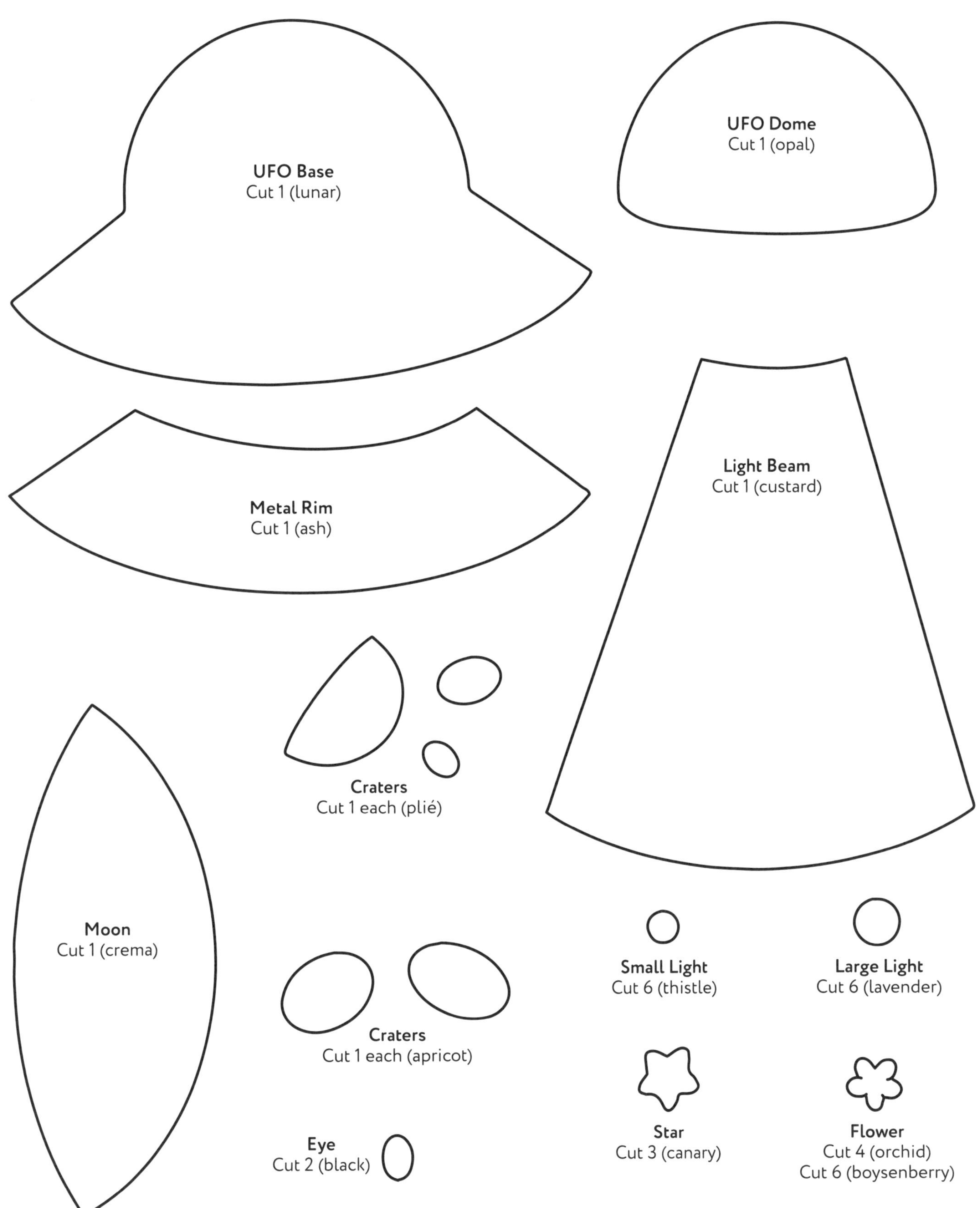
UFO Base
Cut 1 (lunar)
UFO Dome
Cut 1 (opal)
Metal Rim
Cut 1 (ash)
Light Beam
Cut 1 (custard)
Craters
Cut 1 each (plié)
Moon
Cut 1 (crema)
Craters
Cut 1 each (apricot)
Small Light
Cut 6 (thistle)
Large Light
Cut 6 (lavender)
Eye
Cut 2 (black)
Star
Cut 3 (canary)
Flower
Cut 4 (orchid)
Cut 6 (boysenberry)

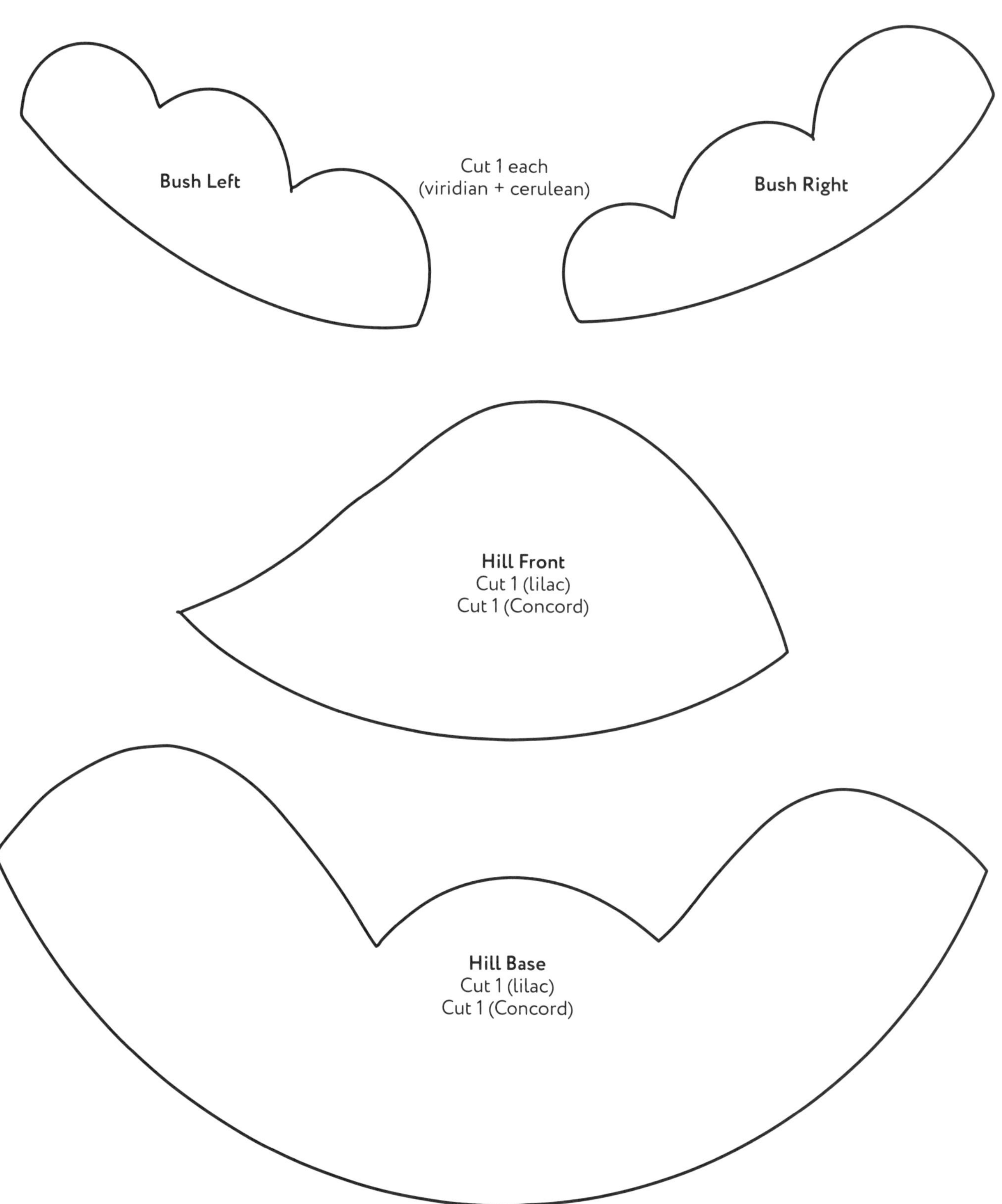
Bush Left
Cut 1 each
(viridian + cerulean)
Bush Right
Hill Front
Cut 1 (lilac)
Cut 1 (Concord)
Hill Base
Cut 1 (lilac)
Cut 1 (Concord)

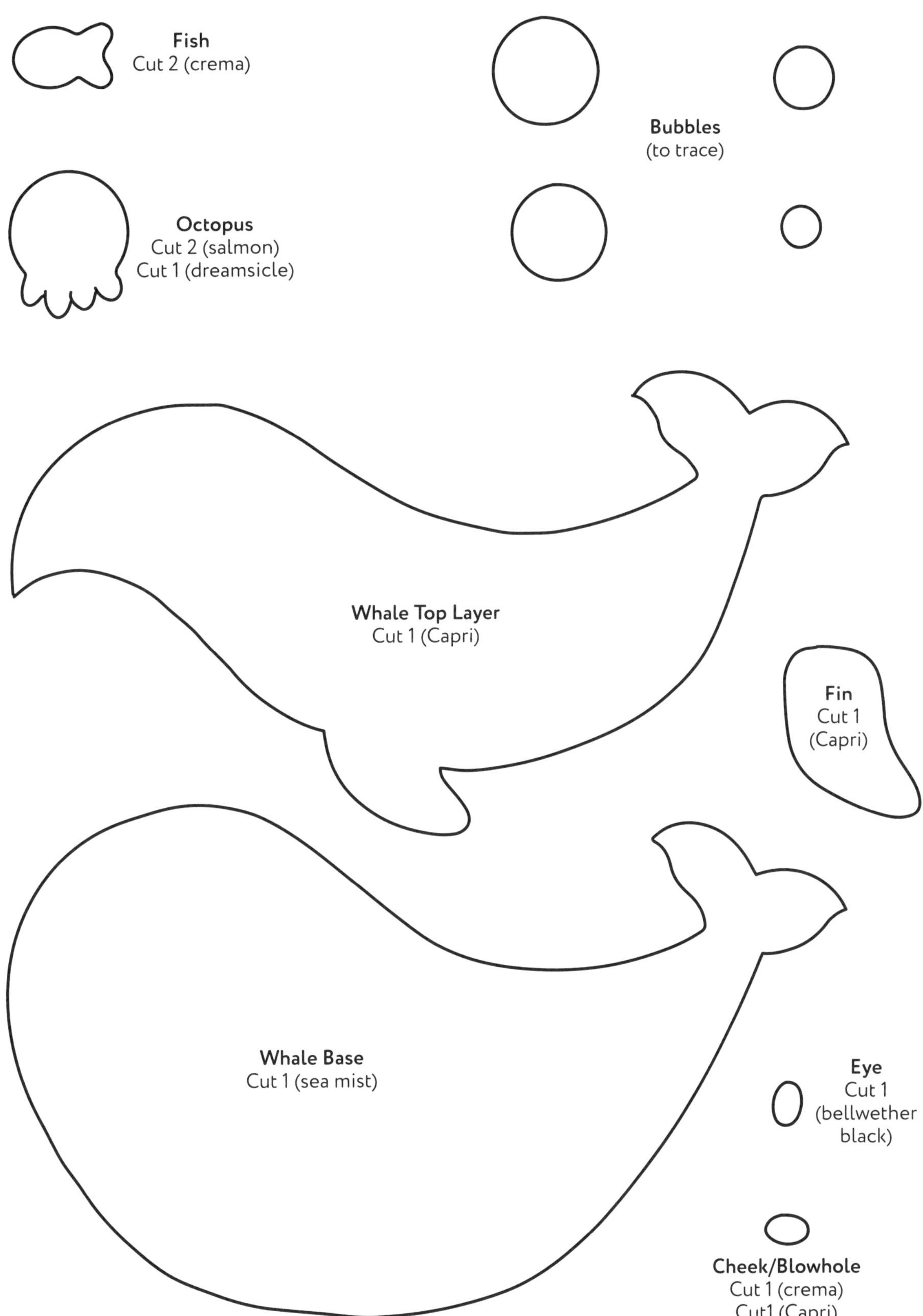
Fish
Cut 2 (crema)
Bubbles
(to trace)
Octopus
Cut 2 (salmon)
Cut 1 (dreamsicle)
Whale Top Layer
Cut 1 (Capri)
Fin
Cut 1
(Capri)
Whale Base
Cut 1 (sea mist)
Eye
Cut 1
(bellwether
black)
Cheek/Blowhole
Cut 1 (crema)
Cut1 (Capri)

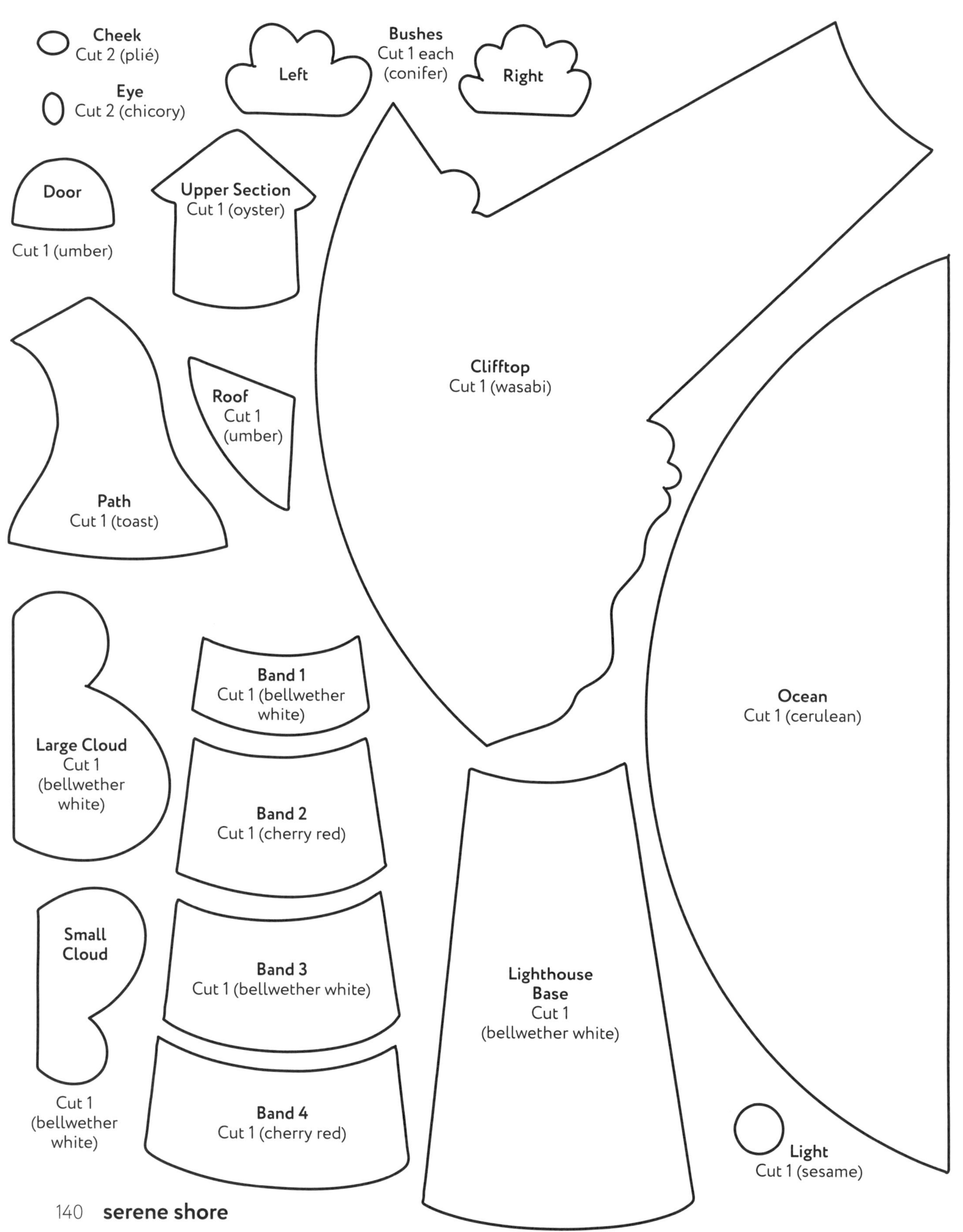
Cheek
Cut 2 (plié)
Eye
Cut 2 (chicory)
Left
Bushes
Cut 1 each
(conifer)
Right
Door
Cut 1 (umber)
Upper Section
Cut 1 (oyster)
Path
Cut 1 (toast)
Roof
Cut 1
(umber)
Clifftop
Cut 1 (wasabi)
Ocean
Cut 1 (cerulean)
Large Cloud
Cut 1
(bellwether
white)
Band 1
Cut 1 (bellwether
white)
Band 2
Cut 1 (cherry red)
Small
Cloud
Cut 1
(bellwether
white)
Band 3
Cut 1 (bellwether white)
Band 4
Cut 1 (cherry red)
Lighthouse
Base
Cut 1
(bellwether white)
Light
Cut 1 (sesame)

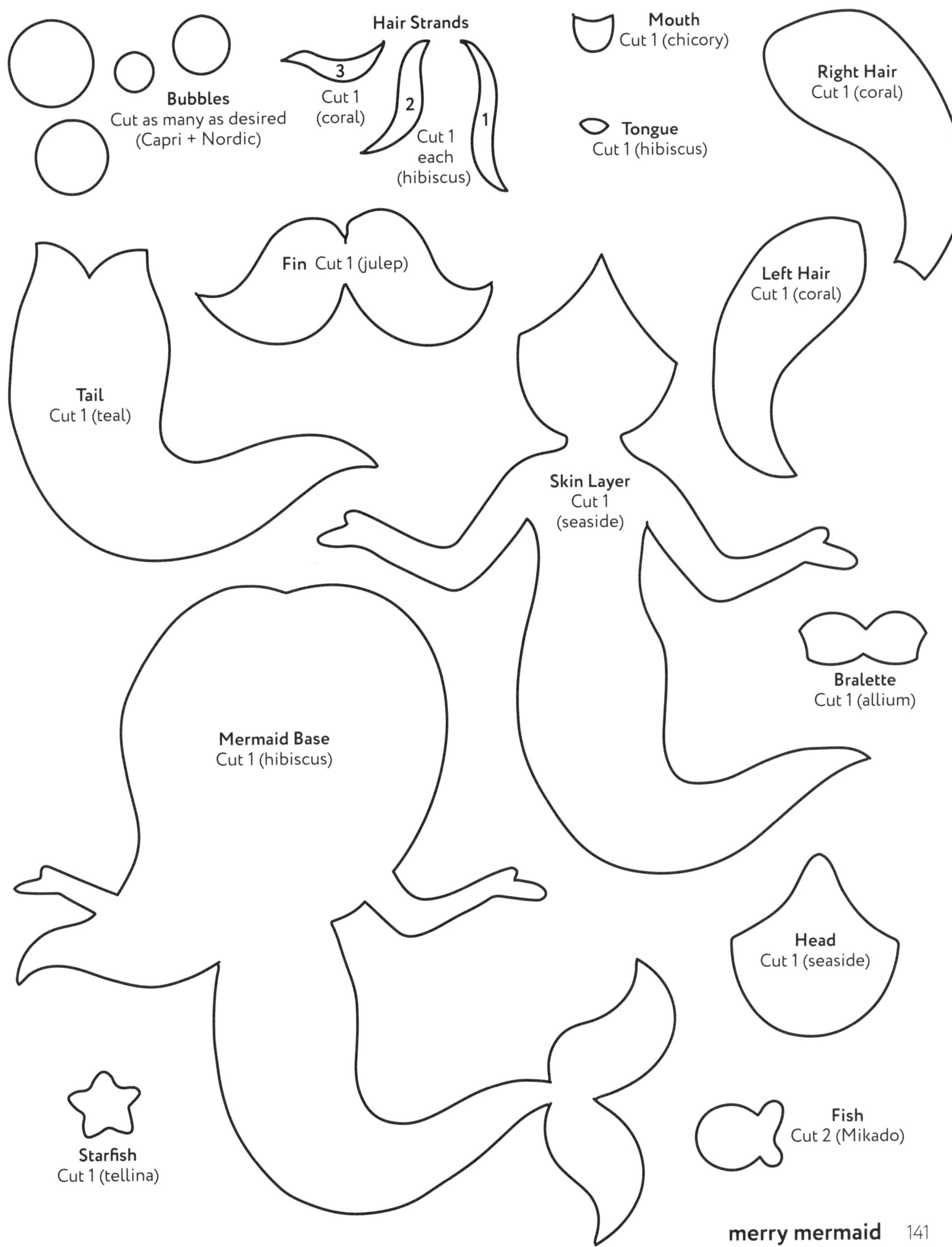
Bubbles
Cut as many as desired
(Capri + Nordic)
Hair Strands
3
Cut 1
(coral)
2
1
Cut 1
each
(hibiscus)
Mouth
Cut 1 (chicory)
Tongue
Cut 1 (hibiscus)
Right Hair
Cut 1 (coral)
Fin Cut 1 (julep)
Left Hair
Cut 1 (coral)
Tail
Cut 1 (teal)
Skin Layer
Cut 1
(seaside)
Bralette
Cut 1 (allium)
Mermaid Base
Cut 1 (hibiscus)
Head
Cut 1 (seaside)
Fish
Cut 2 (Mikado)
Starfish
Cut 1 (tellina)

Taillight
Cut 1 (tellina)
Headlight
Cut 1 (sesame)
Wheel Rim
Cut 2 (golden)
Wheel Base
Cut 2
(bellwether
black)
Taco Meat
Cut 1 (hazelnut)
Eye
Cut 2
(bellwether
black)
Cheek
Cut 2 (coral)
Mouth
Cut 1
(bellwether black)
Taco Shell
Cut 1 (golden)
Taco Lettuce
Cut 1 (citron)
Truck
Lower Half
Cut 1
(dreamsicle)
Post
Cut 2
(bellwether
white)
Truck Base
Cut 1 (clementine)

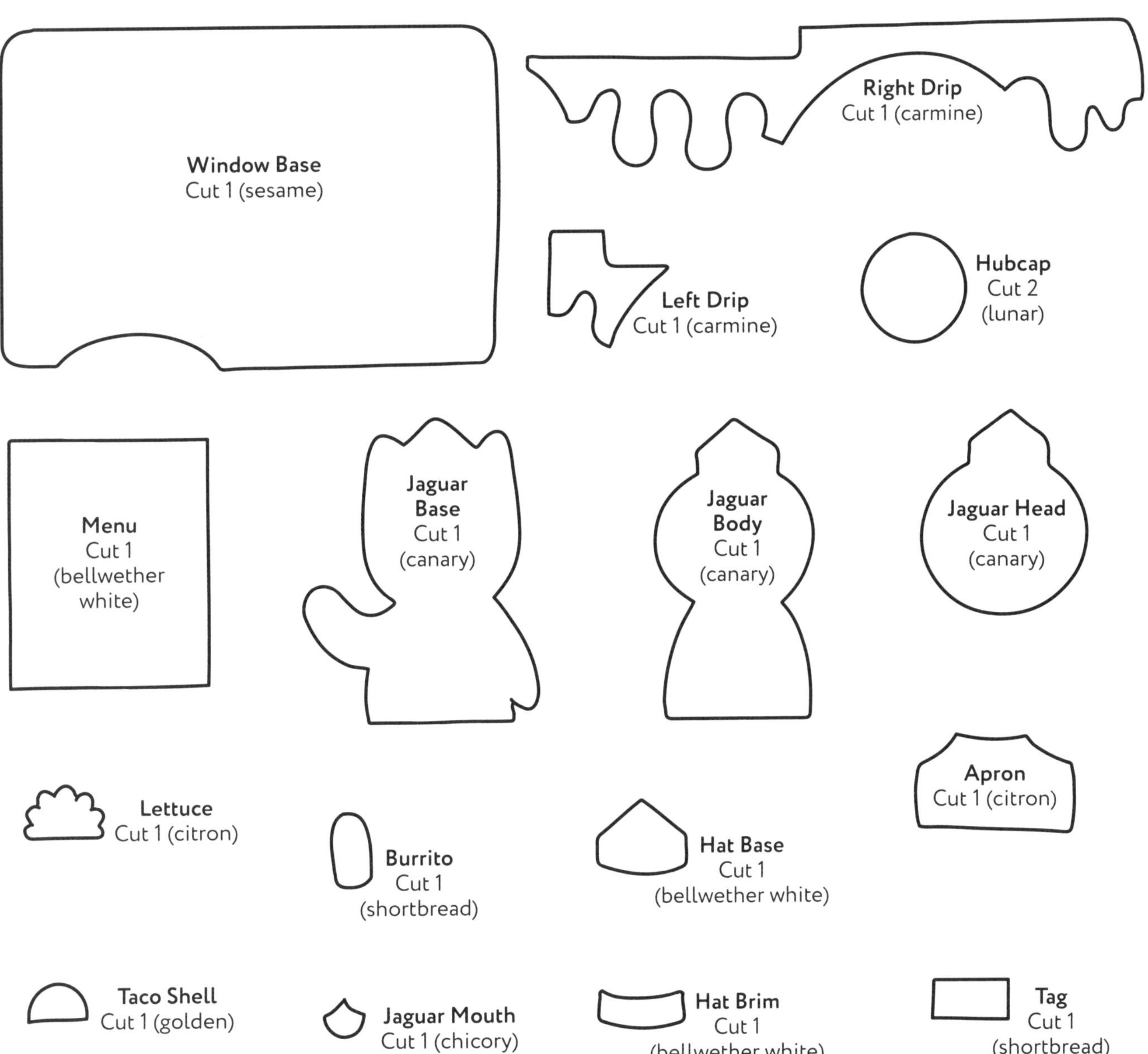
Window Base
Cut 1 (sesame)
Right Drip
Cut 1 (carmine)
Left Drip
Cut 1 (carmine)
Hubcap
Cut 2
(lunar)
Menu
Cut 1
(bellwether
white)
Jaguar
Base
Cut 1
(canary)
Jaguar
Body
Cut 1
(canary)
Jaguar Head
Cut 1
(canary)
Apron
Cut 1 (citron)
Lettuce
Cut 1 (citron)
Burrito
Cut 1
(shortbread)
Hat Base
Cut 1
(bellwether white)
Taco Shell
Cut 1 (golden)
Jaguar Mouth
Cut 1 (chicory)
Hat Brim
Cut 1
(bellwether white)
Tag
Cut 1
(shortbread)

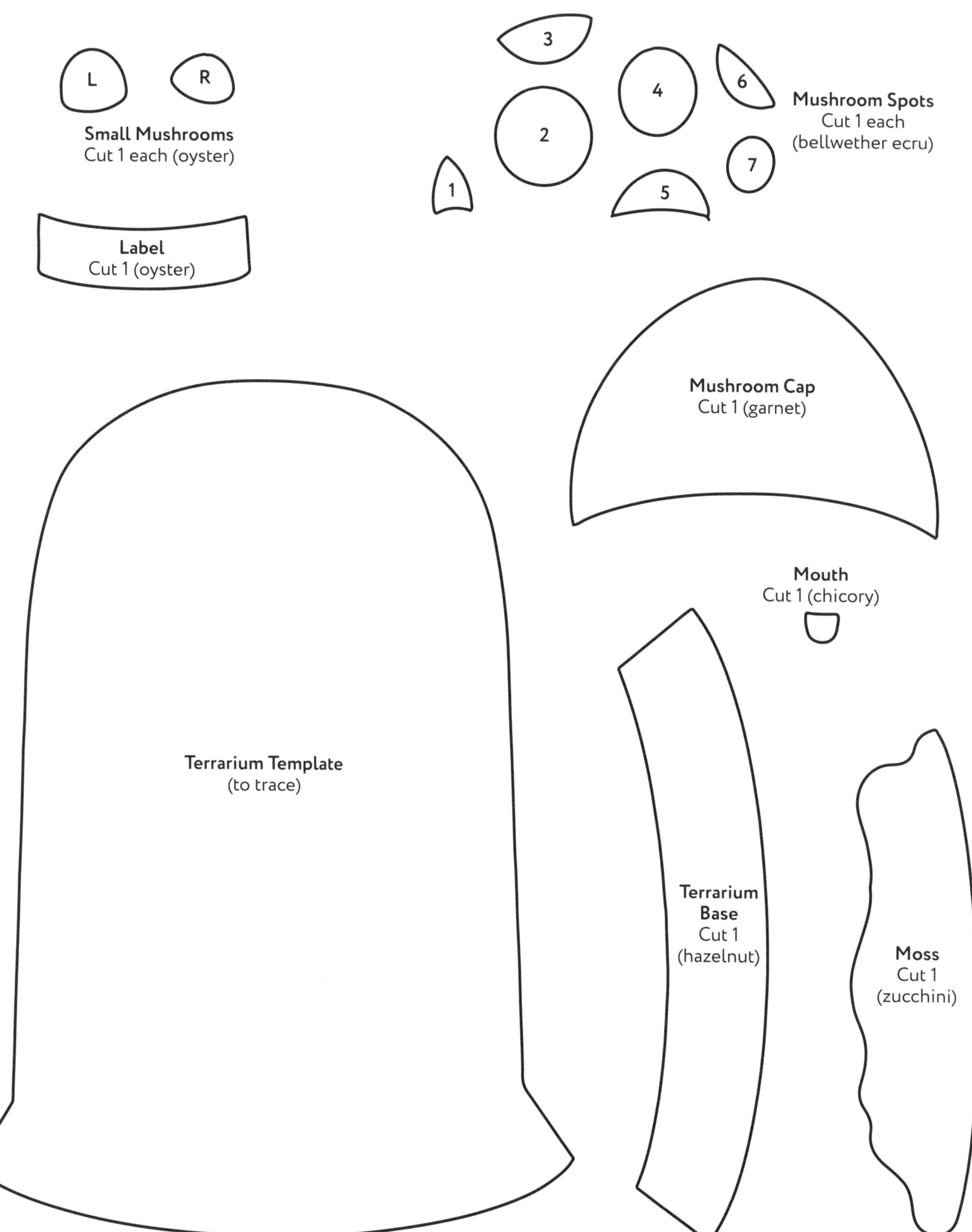
L
R
Small Mushrooms
Cut 1 each (oyster)
3
4
6
2
1
7
5
Mushroom Spots
Cut 1 each
(bellwether ecru)
Label
Cut 1 (oyster)
Mushroom Cap
Cut 1 (garnet)
Mouth
Cut 1 (chicory)
Terrarium Template
(to trace)
Terrarium
Base
Cut 1
(hazelnut)
Moss
Cut 1
(zucchini)

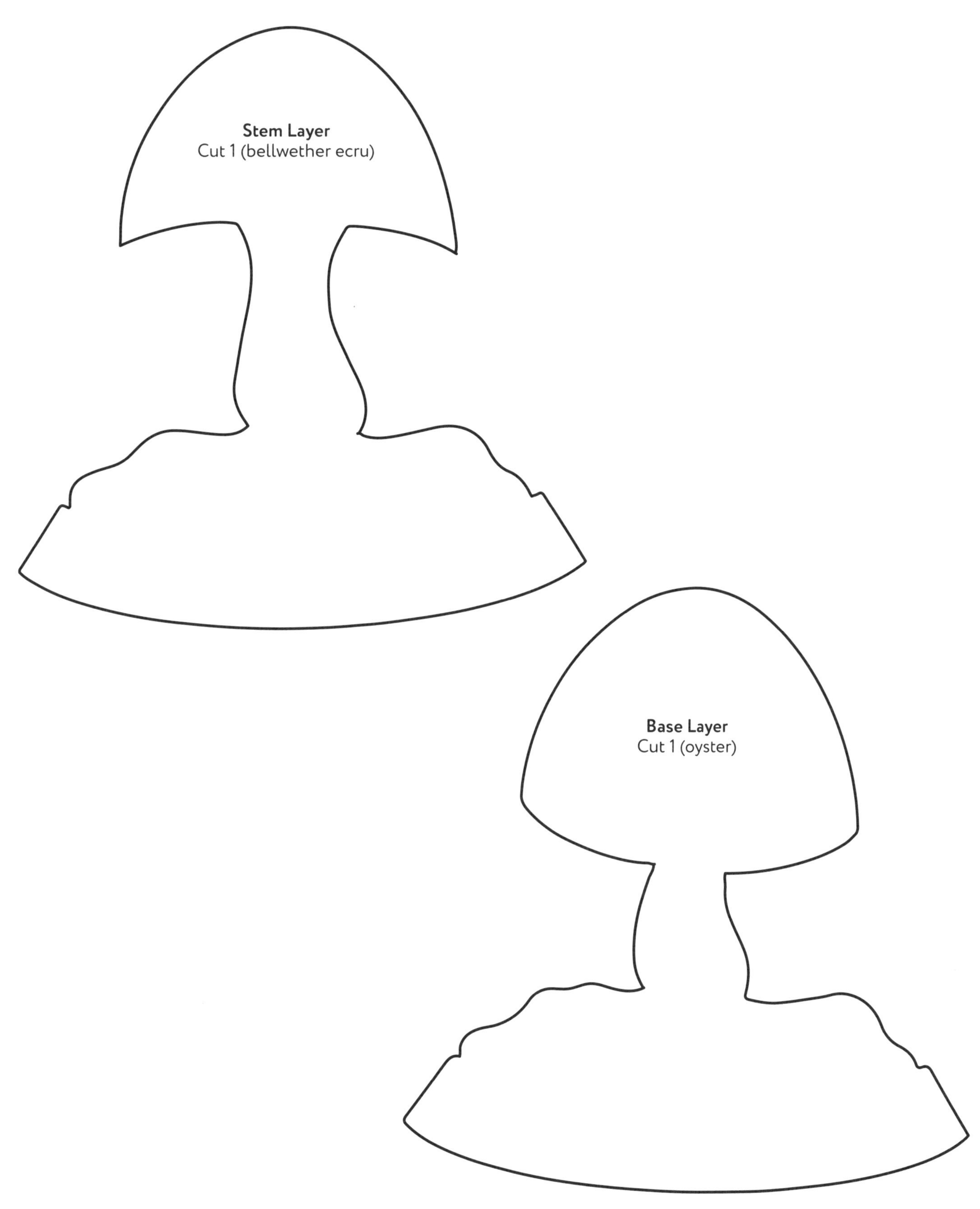
Stem Layer
Cut 1 (bellwether ecru)
Base Layer
Cut 1 (oyster)

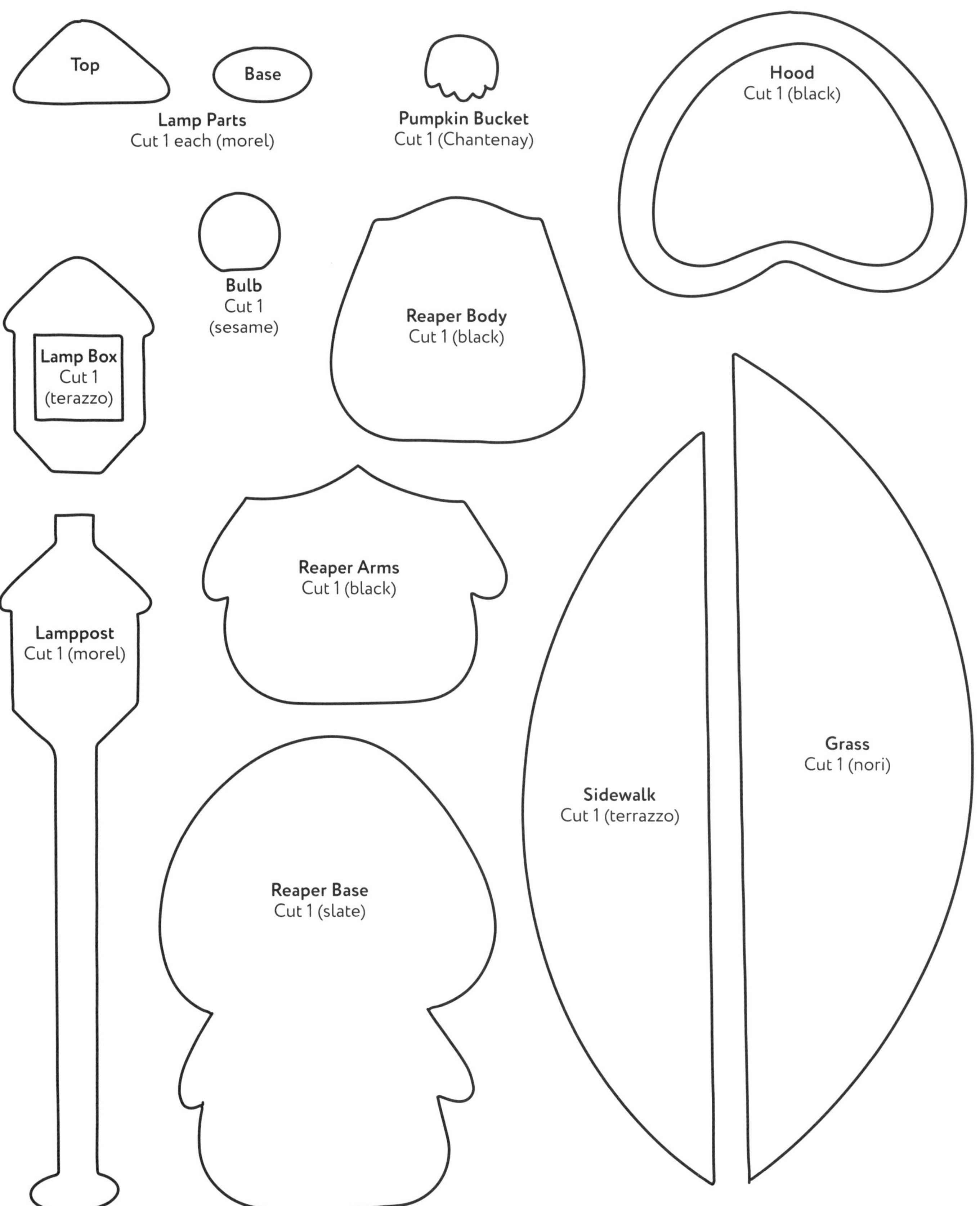
Top
Base
Lamp Parts
Cut 1 each (morel)
Pumpkin Bucket
Cut 1 (Chantenay)
Hood
Cut 1 (black)
Bulb
Cut 1
(sesame)
Lamp Box
Cut 1
(terazzo)
Reaper Body
Cut 1 (black)
Reaper Arms
Cut 1 (black)
Lamppost
Cut 1 (morel)
Grass
Cut 1 (nori)
Sidewalk
Cut 1 (terrazzo)
Reaper Base
Cut 1 (slate)

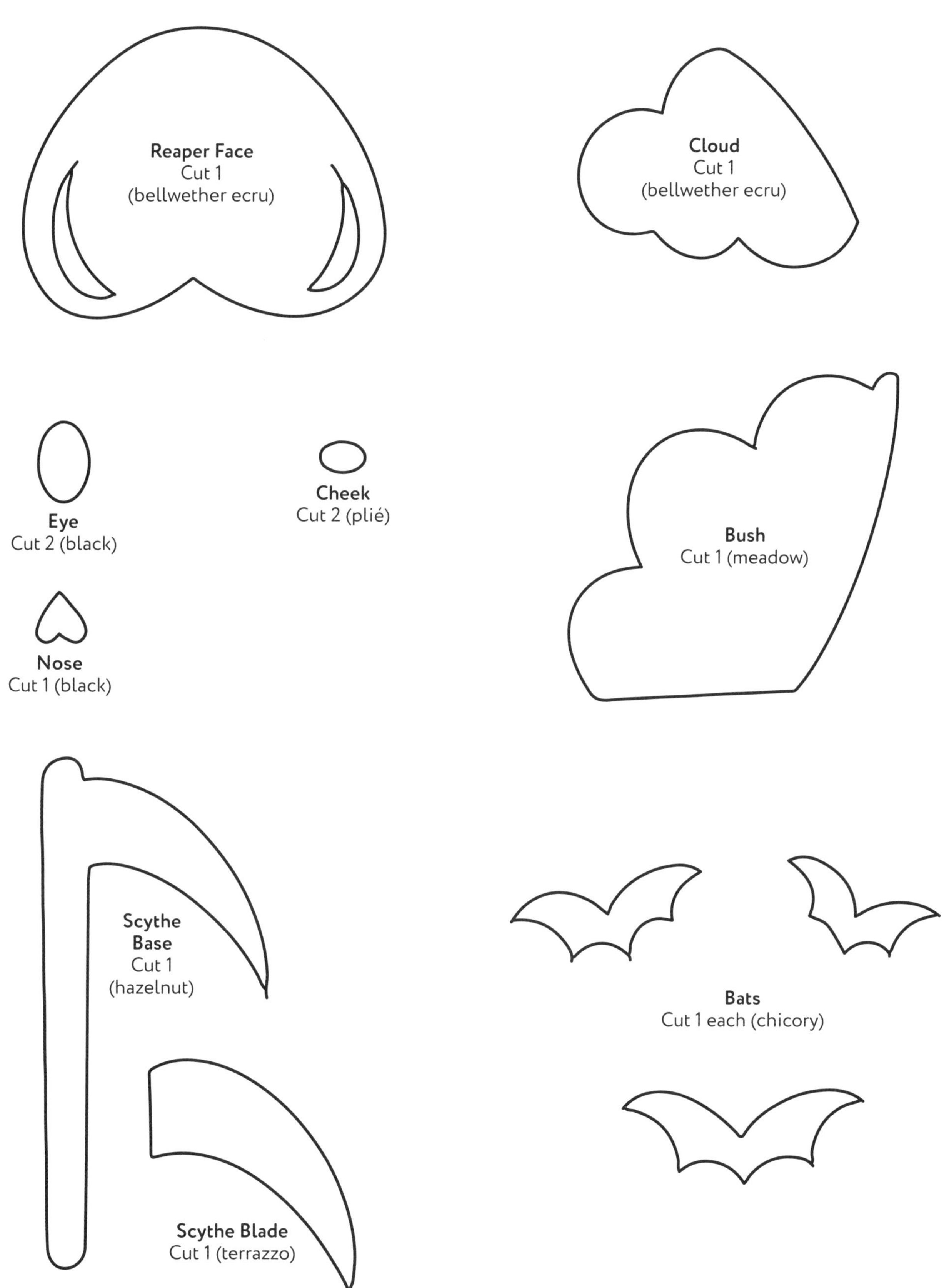
Reaper Face
Cut 1
(bellwether ecru)
Cloud
Cut 1
(bellwether ecru)
Eye
Cut 2 (black)
Cheek
Cut 2 (plié)
Bush
Cut 1 (meadow)
Nose
Cut 1 (black)
Scythe
Base
Cut 1
(hazelnut)
Bats
Cut 1 each (chicory)
Scythe Blade
Cut 1 (terrazzo)

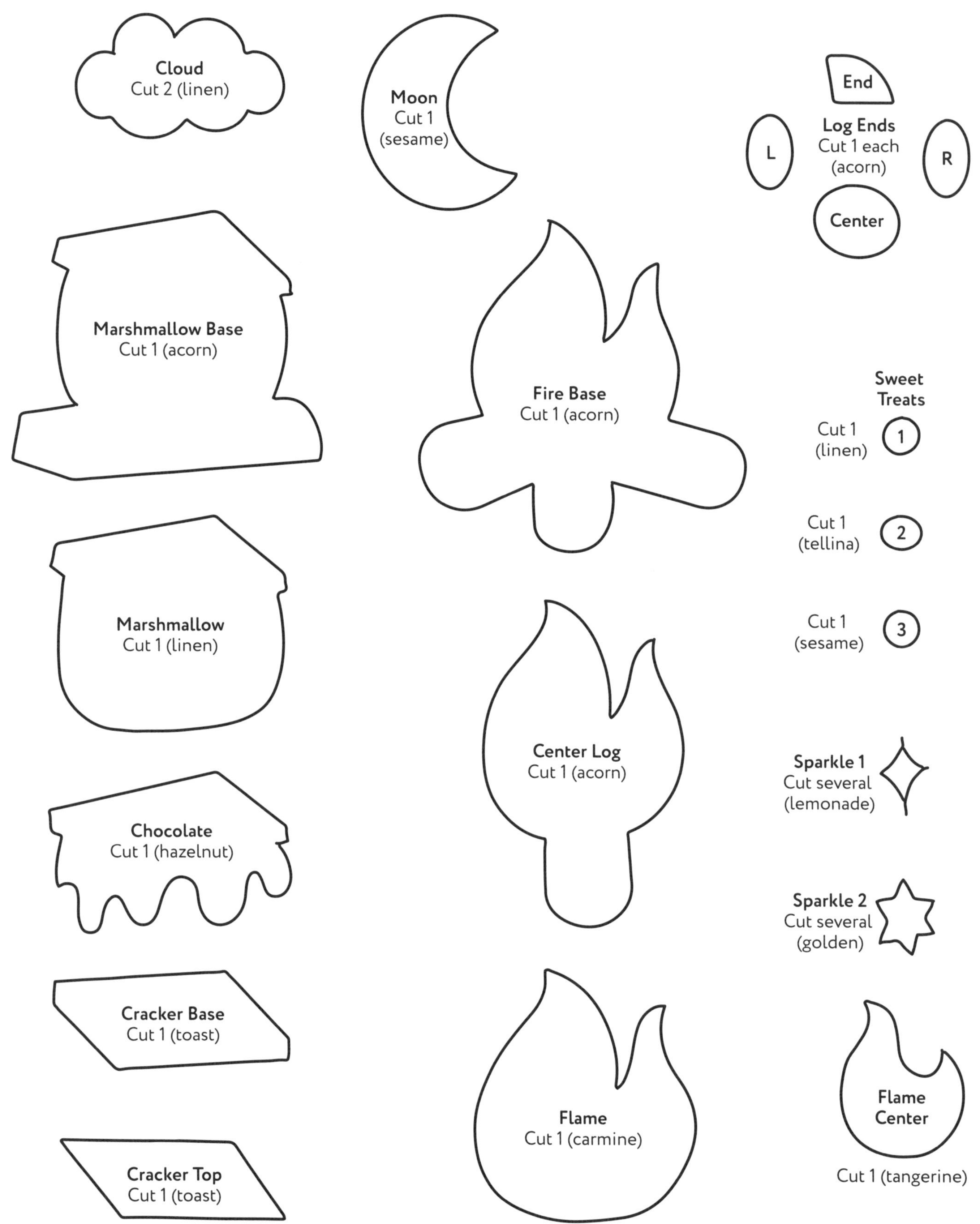
Cloud
Cut 2 (linen)
Moon
Cut 1
(sesame)
End
Log Ends
Cut 1 each
(acorn)
L
R
Center
Marshmallow Base
Cut 1 (acorn)
Fire Base
Cut 1 (acorn)
Sweet
Treats
Cut 1
(linen)
1
Cut 1
(tellina)
2
Marshmallow
Cut 1 (linen)
Cut 1
(sesame)
3
Center Log
Cut 1 (acorn)
Sparkle 1
Cut several
(lemonade)
Chocolate
Cut 1 (hazelnut)
Sparkle 2
Cut several
(golden)
Cracker Base
Cut 1 (toast)
Flame
Cut 1 (carmine)
Flame
Center
Cut 1 (tangerine)
Cracker Top
Cut 1 (toast)

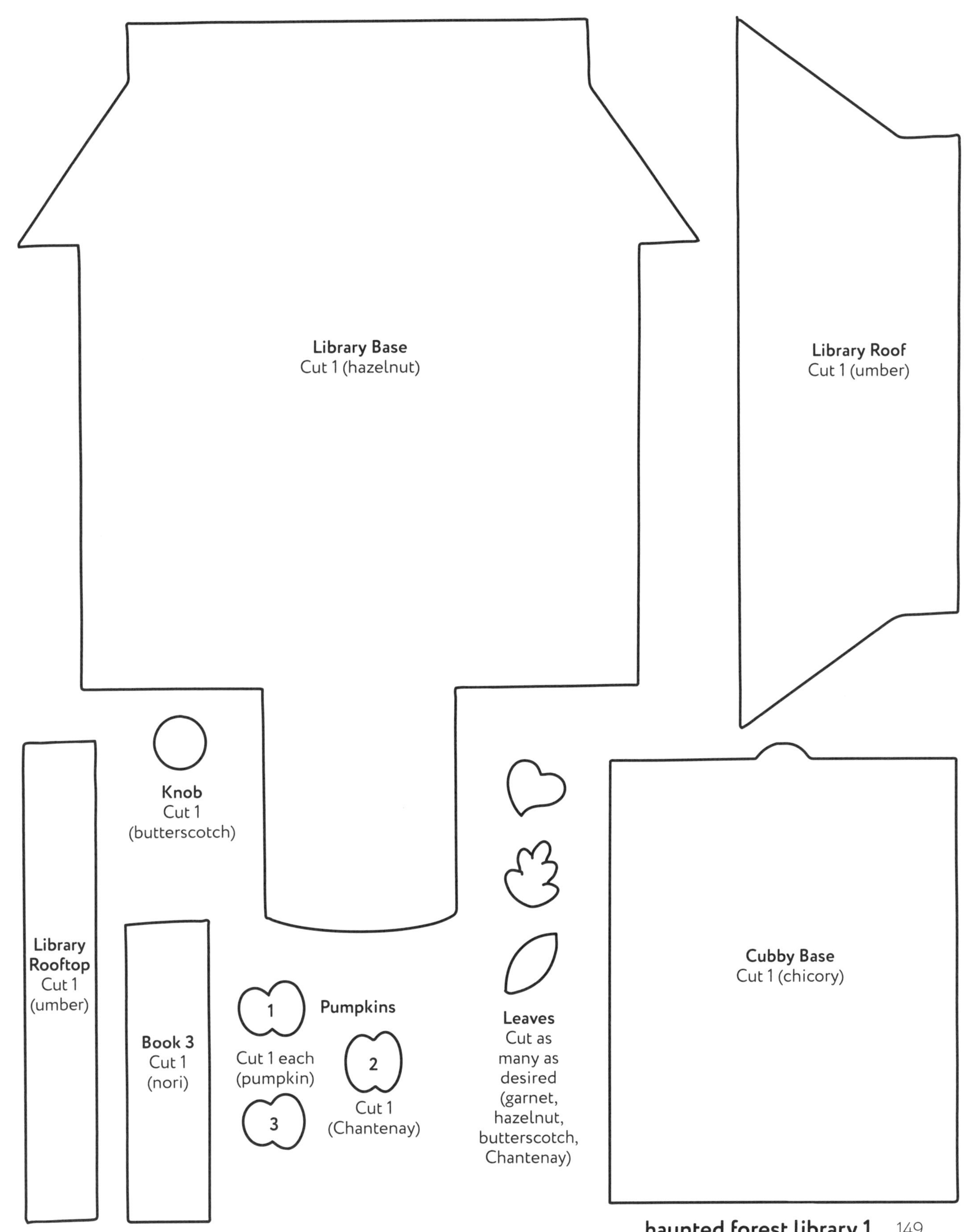

Library Base
Cut 1 (hazelnut)
Library Roof
Cut 1 (umber)
Knob
Cut 1
(butterscotch)
Library Rooftop
Cut 1
(umber)
Book 3
Cut 1
(nori)
1
Pumpkins
Cut 1 each
(pumpkin)
2
3
Cut 1
(Chantenay)
Leaves
Cut as many as desired
(garnet, hazelnut, butterscotch, Chantenay)
Cubby Base
Cut 1 (chicory)

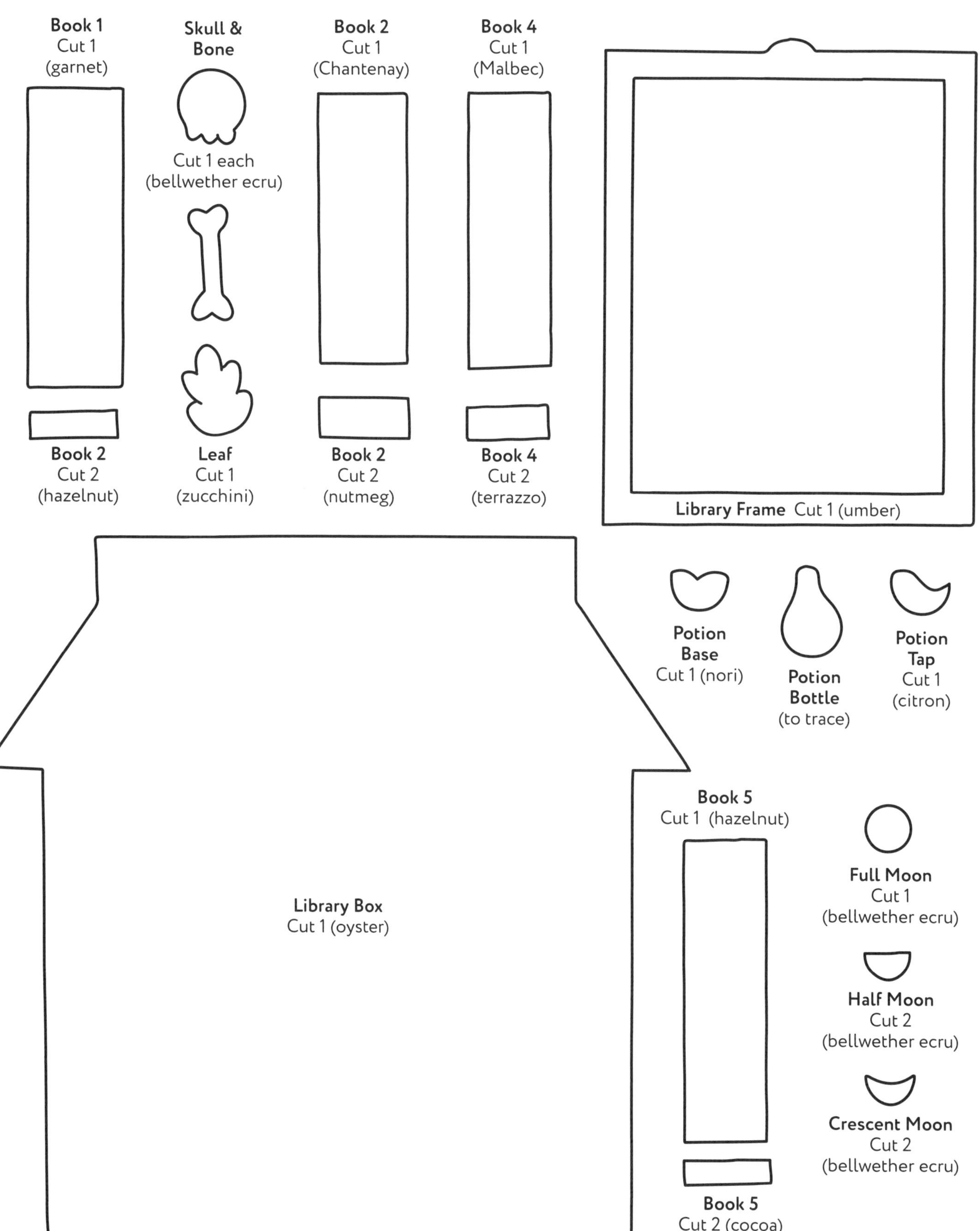
Book 1
Cut 1
(garnet)
Skull &
Bone
Cut 1 each
(bellwether ecru)
Book 2
Cut 1
(Chantenay)
Book 4
Cut 1
(Malbec)
Book 2
Cut 2
(hazelnut)
Leaf
Cut 1
(zucchini)
Book 2
Cut 2
(nutmeg)
Book 4
Cut 2
(terrazzo)
Library Frame Cut 1 (umber)
Potion
Base
Cut 1 (nori)
Potion
Bottle
(to trace)
Potion
Tap
Cut 1
(citron)
Library Box
Cut 1 (oyster)
Book 5
Cut 1 (hazelnut)
Full Moon
Cut 1
(bellwether ecru)
Half Moon
Cut 2
(bellwether ecru)
Crescent Moon
Cut 2
(bellwether ecru)
Book 5
Cut 2 (cocoa)

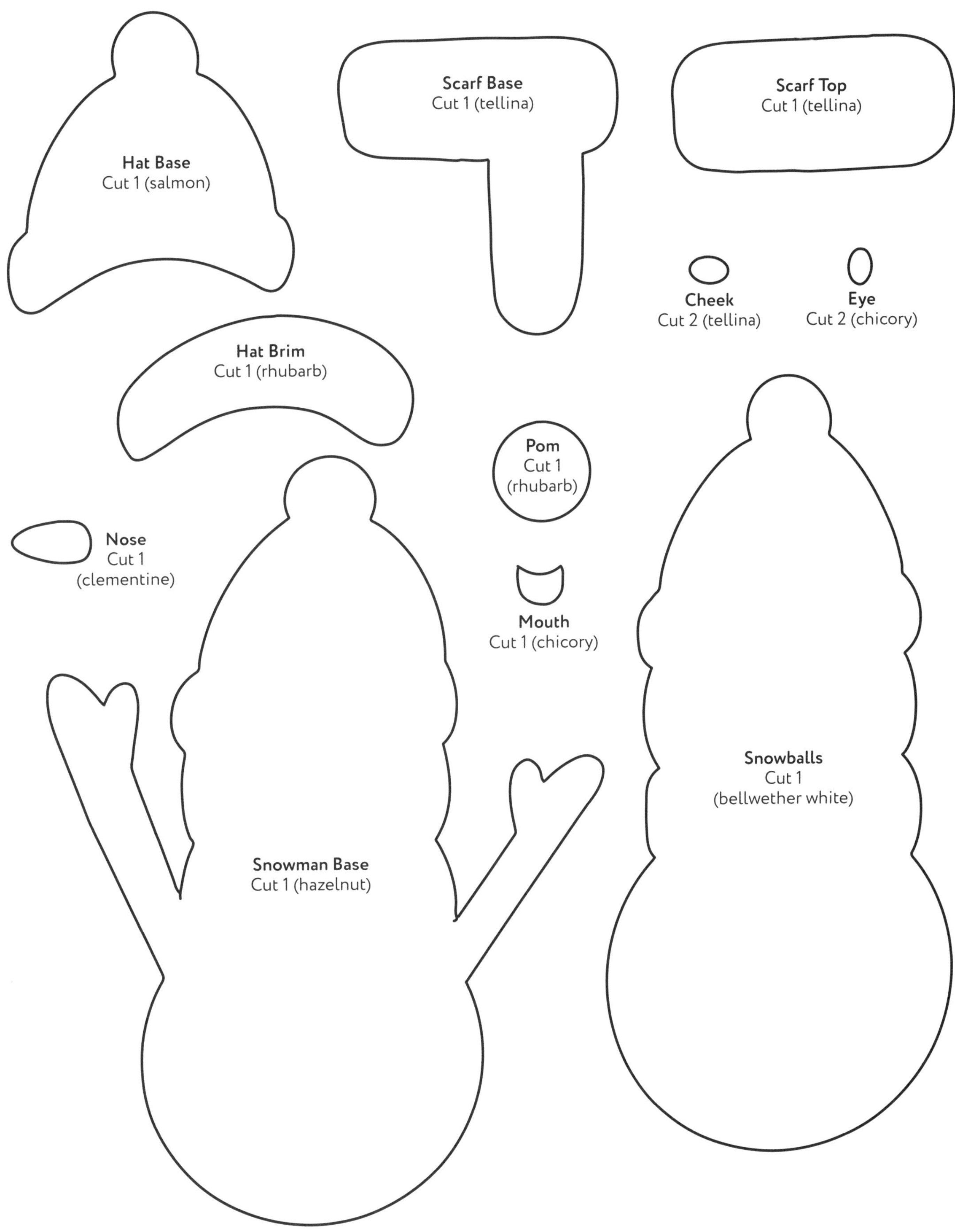
Hat Base
Cut 1 (salmon)
Scarf Base
Cut 1 (tellina)
Scarf Top
Cut 1 (tellina)
Cheek
Cut 2 (tellina)
Eye
Cut 2 (chicory)
Hat Brim
Cut 1 (rhubarb)
Pom
Cut 1
(rhubarb)
Nose
Cut 1
(clementine)
Mouth
Cut 1 (chicory)
Snowballs
Cut 1
(bellwether white)
Snowman Base
Cut 1 (hazelnut)

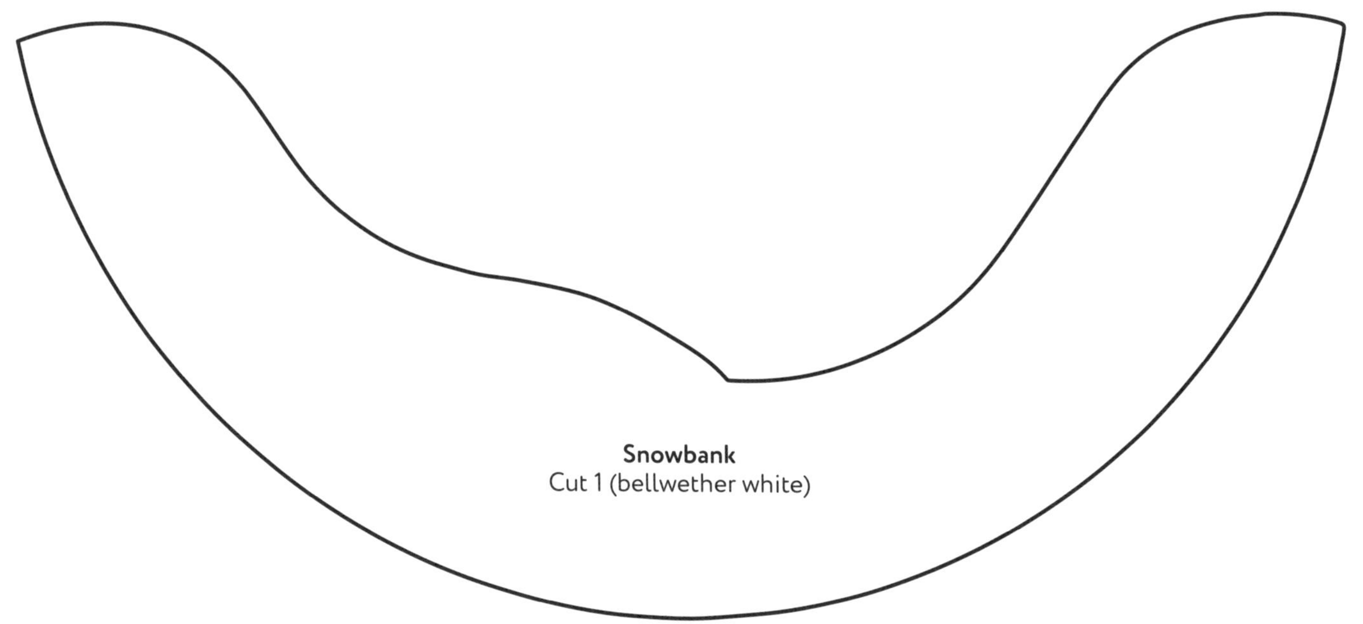
Snowbank
Cut 1 (bellwether white)

Windowsill
Cut 1 (hazelnut)
Gift Box
Cut 1 (viridian)
1
2
3
4
Snow
Cut 1 each (bellwether white)
Tree Line
Cut 1 (evergreen)
Cat Body
Cut 1 (Chantenay)
Cat Head
Cut 1 each (Chantenay)
Back Leg
Front Leg
Stripes
Cut 1 each (umber)
Nose
Cut 1 (umber)
Window Frame
Cut 1 (hazelnut)

Santa Base
Cut 1 (seaside)
Hat
Cut 1 (cherry red)
Cuff
Hat Brim
Cut 1 each
(bellwether white)
Glove
Cut 1
(hazelnut)
Beard
Sleigh
Cut 1 (garnet)
Sleeve
Cut 1 (cherry red)
Reindeer Base
Cut 1 (nutmeg)
Reindeer Top
Cut 1 (nutmeg)
Window Base
Cut 1 (Orion)
Gift-Box Ribbon
Cut 1
(bellwether ecru)

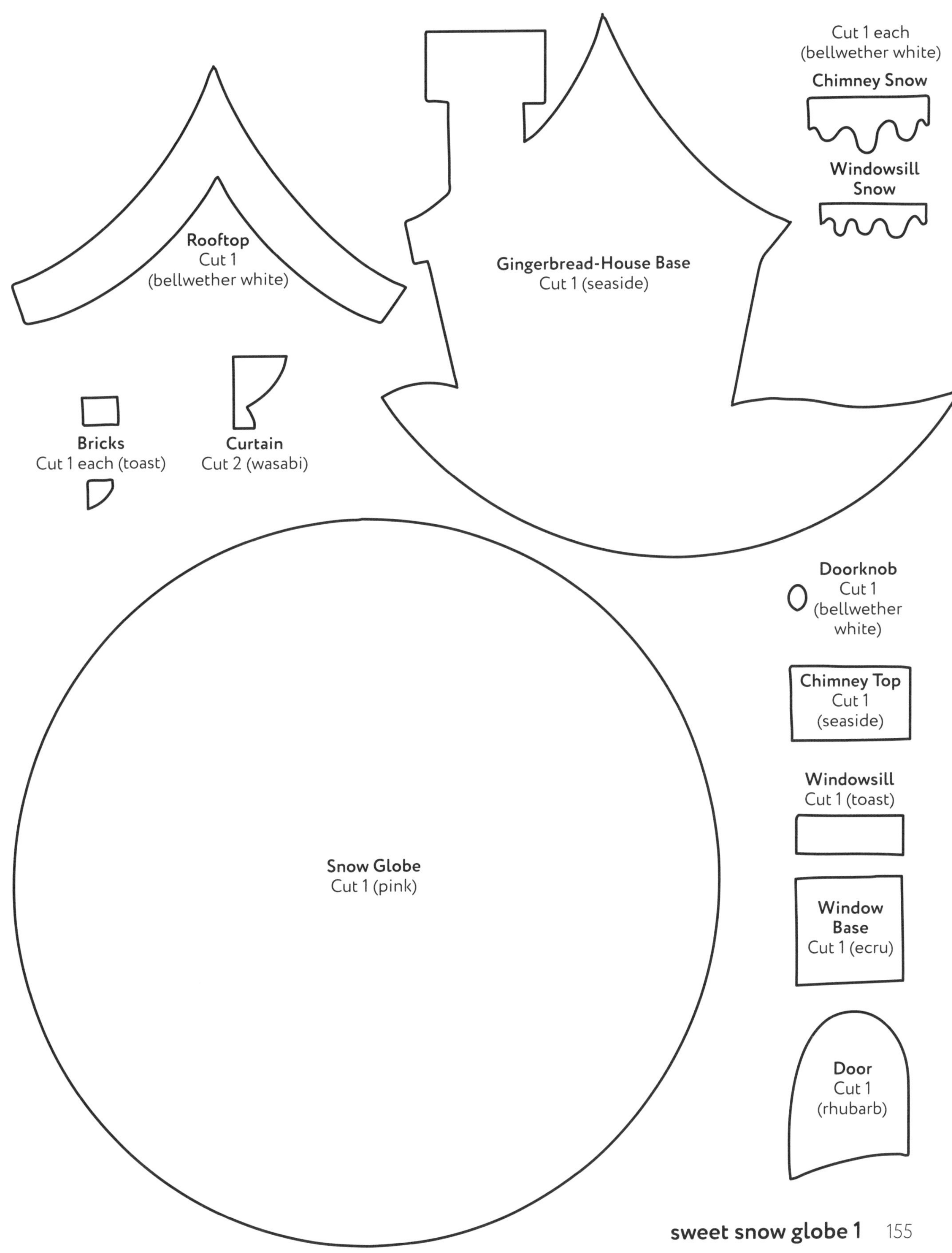
Cut 1 each
(bellwether white)
Chimney Snow
Windowsill
Snow
Rooftop
Cut 1
(bellwether white)
Gingerbread-House Base
Cut 1 (seaside)
Bricks
Cut 1 each (toast)
Curtain
Cut 2 (wasabi)
Doorknob
Cut 1
(bellwether
white)
Chimney Top
Cut 1
(seaside)
Windowsill
Cut 1 (toast)
Snow Globe
Cut 1 (pink)
Window
Base
Cut 1 (ecru)
Door
Cut 1
(rhubarb)

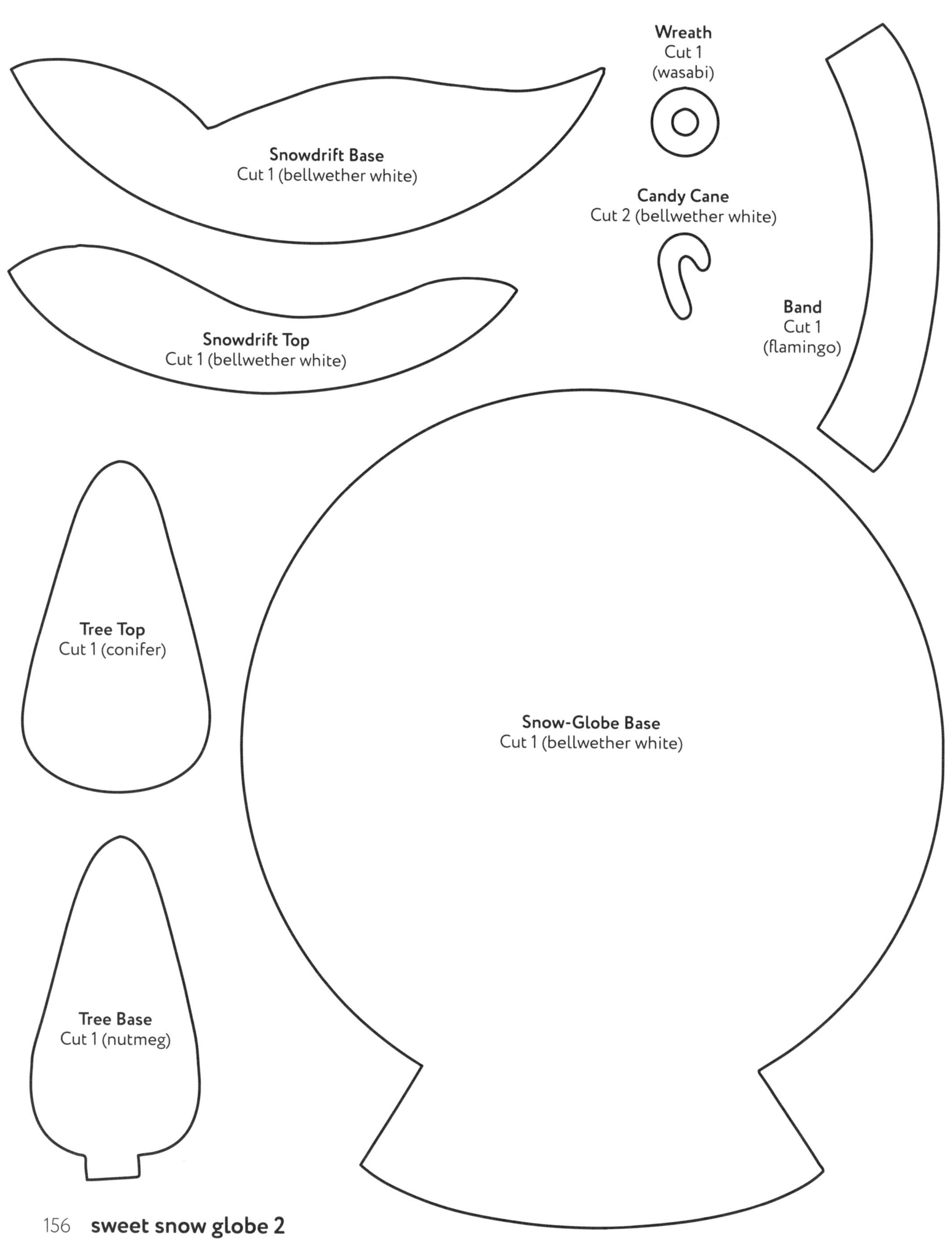
Wreath
Cut 1
(wasabi)
Snowdrift Base
Cut 1 (bellwether white)
Candy Cane
Cut 2 (bellwether white)
Snowdrift Top
Cut 1 (bellwether white)
Band
Cut 1
(flamingo)
Tree Top
Cut 1 (conifer)
Snow-Globe Base
Cut 1 (bellwether white)
Tree Base
Cut 1 (nutmeg)

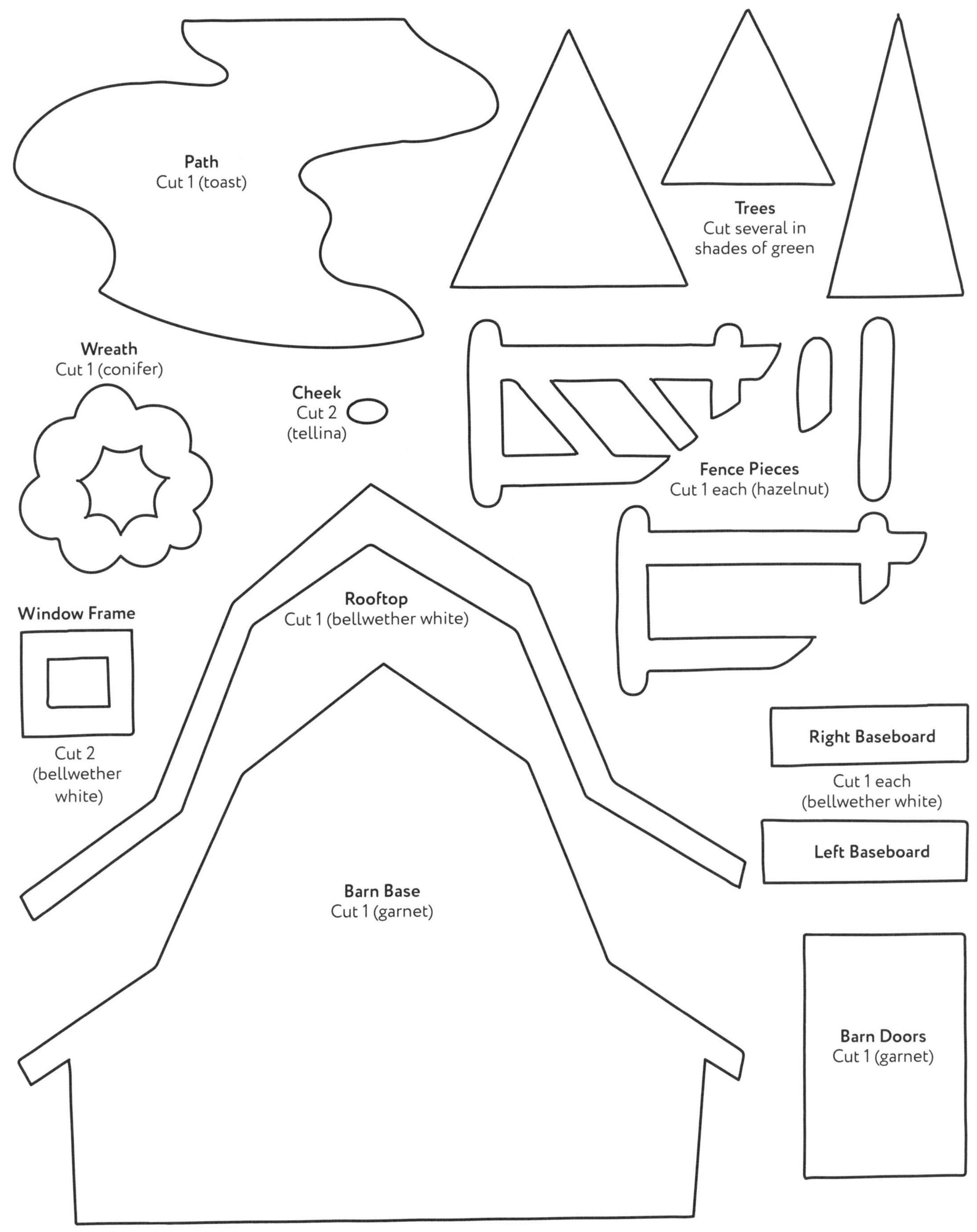
Path
Cut 1 (toast)
Trees
Cut several in
shades of green
Wreath
Cut 1 (conifer)
Cheek
Cut 2
(tellina)
Fence Pieces
Cut 1 each (hazelnut)
Rooftop
Cut 1 (bellwether white)
Window Frame
Cut 2
(bellwether
white)
Right Baseboard
Cut 1 each
(bellwether white)
Left Baseboard
Barn Base
Cut 1 (garnet)
Barn Doors
Cut 1 (garnet)

Index

Page reference key: *italics* indicate projects; **bold** indicates tips for working with kids; (parentheses) indicate templates; asterisks (*) indicate floss color chart.

Acknowledgments

Becoming a published author has been a dream of mine since I was nine years old. While the process of actually writing an entire book has certainly been a lot of work, I can honestly say that my experience was easy and enjoyable thanks to all the people in my corner.

To Charlie, thank you for being the most supportive partner I could have ever asked for. Thank you for all the encouragement, all the delighted squeals over my artwork, and your willingness to take over housework or kiddo care with enthusiasm so that I could get a little bit more work done. I am my best self because of you, and I'll still be loving you when we're stardust.

To my kids (including the teensy one who decided that the perfect time to join our family was right as Mama started writing a book), thank you for being so understanding and patient on days when I didn't have as much time for play. Your pride in my accomplishments has been the very best motivator, and I'm so glad I get to be your mama!

To my extended family, thank you for always encouraging me to follow my dreams. I've never once doubted my ability to do anything I wanted to, and that's largely because of you. Thank you for being so willing to step in and help out with whatever we needed while I worked on this enormous and incredible project.

To Peg, Kaylee, and the entire team at Better Day Books, thank you so much for being as excited about my work as I am. Your warmth, kindness, and care for me throughout this entire process has been truly delightful, and I'm so thankful to be a member of the Better Day family.

To Kate, Logan, and Megan, thank you for cheering me on in literally everything I do, but especially this. I would be truly lost without the three of you. To Jenny, Meg, Rebekah, Erin, Aly, Ashley, Hilary, Em, Iris, and Jessica, I'm so thankful for all your support and insight into publishing, specifically craft books. Doing big things feels a lot less overwhelming with company.

A special thank-you to Renae, Crystal, and the Benzie Design team for supplying most of the materials for the projects in this book. It's an honor to be part of the Benzie family! Thank you to Jaycee of Stay at Home Artist for supplying the most-gorgeous embroidery hoops, and to Kate of Modern Hoopla for the absolutely stunning frames and displays. Your support and generosity mean the world.

And finally, thank YOU for picking up this book. I hope you take the skills you learn here and make some magic.

BETTER DAY BOOKS®

HAPPY • CREATIVE • CURATED

Business is personal at Better Day Books. We were founded on the belief that all people are creative and that making things by hand is inherently good for us. It's important to us that you know how much we appreciate your support. The book you are holding in your hands was crafted with the artistic passion of the author and brought to life by a team of wildly enthusiastic creatives who believed it could inspire you. If it did, please drop us a line and let us know about it. Connect with us on Instagram, post a photo of your art, and let us know what other creative pursuits you are interested in learning about. It all matters to us. You're kind of a big deal.

it's a good day to have a better day!®

www.betterdaybooks.com

better_day_books